WOODLAWN

One Hope. One Dream. One Way.

TODD GERELDS

with Mark Schlabach

HOWARD BOOKS
AN IMPRINT OF SIMON & SCHUSTER, INC.

New York   Nashville   London   Toronto   Sydney   New Delhi

Howard Books
An Imprint of Simon & Schuster, Inc.
1230 Avenue of the Americas
New York, NY 10020

First Howard Books trade paperback edition September 2015

HOWARD and colophon are trademarks of Simon & Schuster, Inc.

For information about special discounts for bulk purchases,
please contact Simon & Schuster Special Sales at 1-866-506-1949
or business@simonandschuster.com.

The Simon & Schuster Speakers Bureau can bring authors
to your live event. For more information or to book an event
contact the Simon & Schuster Speakers Bureau at 1-866-248-3049
or visit our website at www.simonspeakers.com.

Manufactured in the United States of America.

10 9 8 7 6 5 4 3 2 1

Library of Congress Cataloging-in-Publication Data is available.

ISBN 978-1-5011-1806-7
ISBN 978-1-5011-1810-4 (ebook)

CONTENTS

FOREWORD

by Bobby Bowden

I grew up in the Woodlawn neighborhood of Birmingham, Alabama. The backyard of my family's home was adjacent to Woodlawn High School's football field. I can still remember hearing the sounds of the marching band and the boys practicing football over the fence from our backyard. On some days, my daddy pulled out a ladder, and he and I would climb on the roof of our garage to watch Woodlawn's football team practice. My daddy loved watching football, and I loved watching it with him. Those autumn days on the roof of the garage with my father are some of my favorite memories.

In the 1940s, Woodlawn High School was the team to beat in the city of Birmingham. In fact, the Colonels were one of the best teams in the state nearly every season. Woodlawn High won three consecutive state championships from 1941 to 1943, winning 27 games in a row in the process. I loved watching Harry Gilmer, who was Woodlawn's star tailback and would become an All-American at the University of Alabama. He was one of the first players to throw a jump pass, and I loved going into our backyard and trying to emulate it.

In January 1943, I was diagnosed with rheumatic fever, which was considered a very serious illness back then. Doctors told my mother that I had an enlarged heart. They ordered me to stay in bed, and I ended up being bedridden for nearly a year. I missed going to school and playing baseball and football with my friends. Every Friday night during the fall, I'd turn on my radio and listen to Woodlawn's football games. It was a brief escape from my illness. At least I could listen to the Colonels and imagine that I was still playing football for a few hours every week.

After spending nearly a year in a bed, I was given clearance by my doctors to return to school. I enrolled at Woodlawn High School in January 1944, but my doctors still wouldn't let me play sports. I was devastated. I joined the Woodlawn High School marching band and performed in the orchestra, but music didn't replace my love for sports. Fortunately, my mother took me to another doctor for a second opinion during my junior year in 1946. He gave me clearance to play sports again. I still remember weeping in his office because I was so happy.

I was able to play football during two seasons at Woodlawn High School. When I was a senior, I was named co-captain of my team, which was a big honor for me. We played in front of crowds of nearly twenty thousand fans at Legion Field, which felt like big-time football to me. I loved playing for Woodlawn High coach Kenny Morgan, who taught me a lot about what it meant to be a man and a leader. I graduated from Woodlawn High School in 1948 and attended Howard College (now Samford University) in Birmingham, where I played baseball and football.

Despite my illness, I wouldn't have traded my childhood for anything. I loved attending Woodlawn High School, where we started every school day with the Pledge of Allegiance and a prayer. Boy, they wouldn't let you do that today, would they? I met my wife, Ann, at Woodlawn High School, and we still get back to Birmingham for our class reunions as often as we can. Some of our closest friends were our classmates at Woodlawn High School. We've always considered Birmingham our home.

After I coached football at South Georgia College, West Virginia University, and then Florida State University, I visited Woodlawn High School on a few occasions to recruit some of its players. During the 1970s, I was fortunate to meet Tandy Gerelds, who coached the Colonels from 1971 to 1975. I knew Tandy was a great football coach. I liked to keep up with Woodlawn High School's progress, and I knew they were winning a lot of games in the early 1970s.

I also knew that Tandy was a man of faith and that he shared many of the same beliefs I have. When I was sick as a child, my mother told me to pray to God and ask Him to heal me. I remember my mother holding me in her arms while I prayed. I made a pledge to God. I told Him that if He healed me and allowed me to play football again, I would serve Him for the rest of my life. He did, and I did . . .

As a football coach for more than sixty years, I thought it was my duty to share the Word of God and be a witness to my players. I believed I had that responsibility as a Christian. Having read about Jesus in the Bible, I learned that we are saved through grace. I realized as a young man that if I accepted Jesus Christ as my Savior and surrendered my life to Him, then I would go to heaven. I learned that He died on the cross for me and for my sins. There is nothing you and I can do to repay Him for that sacrifice, so we accept Him as our Savior.

I wanted the boys I coached to understand faith. More than anything, I wanted them to be good men, fathers, and husbands;

and I wanted them to love their fellow teammates and fellow citizens—both black and white.

I'm proud to know that Tandy Gerelds and his coaches felt the same way about their players. The civil rights struggle was one of the darkest chapters in America's history, and Birmingham was one of the most intense battlegrounds. During the early 1970s, Woodlawn High School was plagued by racial strife after government-mandated busing brought hundreds of African American students to its campus. It was the first time white and black students attended Woodlawn High together. It was a new experience, and the kids didn't know how to relate to each other.

And of course, the racial problems extended to Woodlawn High School's football team. Tandy Gerelds and his coaches had to teach their players how to get along and play with each other. He had to teach his kids how to become a *team* and how to trust and love each other. Through the salvation of Jesus Christ, Tandy found the way to bring these boys together in 1973. What transpired over the next couple of seasons was nothing short of a miracle. That's the legacy of Tandy Gerelds and Woodlawn High School.

—Tallahassee, Florida, May 2015

PREFACE

by Todd Gerelds

On a cold winter day, I looked out at the packed sanctuary of First Baptist Church in Tuscumbia, Alabama. People were literally standing in the aisles, against the walls, out into the lobby, and out the front door. I was eulogizing my father, Tandy Gerelds. He had died a week earlier on January 10, 2003, after battling cancer for nearly six months.

My family and I were living in Perkasie, Pennsylvania, when I received the tearful call from my mother. I had seen my dad just about a week earlier when we'd gone home for an extended visit over the Christmas holidays. We left my parents' home on January 2, and Dad died eight days later.

At his funeral, I had the privilege and honor of talking about him to hundreds of people. I saw people from the little town of Tuscumbia. I saw people from the even smaller town called Belmont, Mississippi. I also recognized a bunch of folks from the large city of Birmingham, Alabama. My dad wasn't a movie star or politician, and he wasn't a best-selling novelist or a famous singer. To me, he was Dad. To the roomful of people, he was best known by another name—"Coach."

Why were so many people drawn to pay their respects to Coach Gerelds? He won a lot of football games and even a state

championship. Was that it? Nope. Was he charming and amaz-
ingly handsome? Well, my mom would say so; but being that I
look a lot like him, I promise you it wasn't his looks. Actually,
"charming" may be the last word anyone would use to describe
my dad (again other than Mom). *So what was it?* That is what I
wanted to share with these people who had come to the church
to comfort my mom and our family.

I told his friends, former players, and former students that
when a room in a church sanctuary in a little town in rural North
Alabama fills up with people to honor someone, it's because of
one thing—love. I shared with them that Dad *truly* loved people.
A few chuckles could be heard above sniffles and sobs when I said
he didn't always come off as very sweet. But if you were fortunate
enough to know the man, there was no doubt about his love for
people. He was a man who spoke truth in love. He told people
what they *needed* to hear, not necessarily what they *wanted* to
hear.

The people who knew Dad the best know that he didn't start
as a man who loved people. Someone changed him and trans-
formed him into a great coach and a great man. Late in his life,
he told me, "I'd love to be more like you with people. But, I just
don't like people that much." I laugh as I write this because it
gives you a glimpse of the personality and natural demeanor my
dad possessed. He was not a naturally gregarious, backslapping,
buddy-buddy type of man. Yet, he deeply loved people. I'm not
saying he always liked people, but he always loved them well—
loving requires something of a person.

So when did this naturally hard, tough, and kind of ornery
guy begin to change into a man who loved so intensely that a
church would overflow with people at his funeral?

The change began at Woodlawn High School during the early 1970s.

When I was a little boy running around the Woodlawn High campus, the magnitude of what was happening in Birmingham during the 1960s and 1970s was lost on me. I wasn't old enough to understand that a civil rights war was being fought in the churches, streets, and schools of Alabama—including Woodlawn. All I knew at the time was that there was a big net filled with foam cushions at the Woodlawn High track, and there was a gym and a weight room. I also knew my dad was a football coach and that his team was named the Woodlawn Colonels.

To me, the players he coached were larger than life. They were always nice to me, and I loved being around them . . . They even called me "Little Coach." When Woodlawn High won its games on Thursday and Friday nights, Dad would let me go into the locker room afterward and celebrate with the players and coaches. Then I'd pile onto the bus with the players and ride back to the school.

As I child, I didn't know that things hadn't always been this way. I didn't know that not too long ago, there was tension between blacks and whites and that they did *not* play together as a team, but rather tried to impede each other's success. By the time I was hanging out with the team, they actually loved each other. The players had different numbers; they played different positions; they even looked different. Some were black and some were white; some were big and some not so big—even though they all seemed pretty big to me at the time. But these differences didn't matter. They all wore green and gold, and they were a team.

Over the years, Dad shared with me more and more of what had transpired at Woodlawn High School, from the start of his coaching career until the day he decided to leave the sideline. I learned that what happened during two magical seasons in 1973 and 1974 could only be described as miraculous. What God did to transform the hearts and minds of students, athletes, parents, coaches, administrators, teachers, and a community of people was truly astonishing.

The early 1970s in America produced a generation of hippies, who were disillusioned with the ruling establishment. In the short span of their lives up to that point, they'd witnessed a U.S. president assassinated and their country mired in a confusing war that never seemed to end in a faraway country. As they made it through their high school years, they watched another U.S. president leave office in disgrace after a scandal, and witnessed the murder of Dr. Martin Luther King, who was truly making a difference in the world for good. The world around them seemed out of control.

The God of the universe is *the* constant in a world of flux. There are times in history when it seems that the human heart is starved for Truth. Our souls ache to be filled with something—or Someone—real. In the 1970s, the "Jesus Freaks" movement was our country's answer to disillusionment. Today, our fascination with "reality television," YouTube, and social media betrays the longings of our hearts that aren't dissimilar to what the youth of 1973 were experiencing. We crave connection. We crave reality. My prayer is that as you read this book, you will realize that the God of the universe *is real* and that He can enter any and every circumstance and do miraculous things. I also hope that you will be encouraged by the certainty that He is the One your heart longs to connect with and that He is eager to connect with you.

Tandy Gerelds was my dad and a beloved coach. He was a

regular guy. Yet the profundity of his life has impressed me more and more as I meet people who knew him. It seems that not a week passes without meeting someone who played for Dad, coached against Dad, or had some sort of connection where God had used my dad in their life.

Dad taught me so much. He taught me about the value of hard work, as I watched his teams work hard every season. He taught me about loyalty, because he always expected his players to be there for one another. He taught me about toughness, as he coached his players to be tough and disciplined. He also taught me about defeat. He taught his team to "leave it all on the field" and let the results take care of themselves. He encouraged us all to walk off the field with our heads held high if we had given our all. And he taught me about truth. He spoke the truth, and he expected complete honesty from others.

Most of all, my dad taught me about love. From the night he met Jesus in Birmingham in 1973 until the night he coached his last game at tiny Belmont High School in 2002, I believe that the boys on his teams played harder because they knew he loved them.

The gravity of moments in our lives is often lost at the time. Years of joys, pains, victories, defeats, and living life are what bring us perspective. Today, forty years removed from those childhood moments, their gravity and impact have become clearer to me. What happened at Woodlawn High School in the early 1970s was *real*. What happened at Woodlawn High was miraculous. What happened at Woodlawn High was true connection and true love. As the years have passed by since Dad died, the impact of his life has become clearer. I realize only now that a regular life touched by the God of the universe has an impact on eternity.

This book is the culmination of much research and many published interviews. In addition to telling the story of my father, Tandy Gerelds, this book also tells stories of the men and women, boys and girls who had a part during the tumultuous 1960s and '70s in the highly segregated city of Birmingham. It tells about the spiritual transformation of my father and of the whole Woodlawn football team, and it tells about the beginning of healing between individuals and throughout a city.

As you'll see in the characters and events in this book, God takes the mundane and makes it spectacular. This is the story of Woodlawn High School. It is the story of Tandy Gerelds. And it's the story of how God transforms hearts and heals longtime wounds. My prayer is that this story will be the story of your life as well.

Grace and Peace,
Birmingham, Alabama, May 2015

CHAPTER ONE

BOMBINGHAM

Just twelve years before the eventful football game at Legion Field in 1974, no one was cheering for two integrated football teams—and certainly not at Woodlawn High. But on the morning of September 2, 1965, six students quietly enrolled for the first day of classes at Woodlawn High School. They were the first African Americans to ever attend classes at the historically lily-white school, which was among the last of the city's public schools to integrate blacks into its student body.

Among these students was a teenager named Cynthia Holder and her two cousins and their three neighbors. Cynthia, who was fifteen years old at the time, was about to begin her junior year, after spending the previous two school years at the all-black Phillips High School. At the beginning of the summer, her cousin and best friend, Rita Eileen King, told Cynthia that she and her brother Cedric were going to integrate Woodlawn High, along with three other students from their church—Myrtice Chamblin, Lily Humphries, and Leon Humphries.

"Rita and I grew up like sisters and were very close," said Holder, who is now Cynthia Holder Davis Thompson and lives in Birmingham. "The other kids and their pastor decided they wanted to integrate Woodlawn High School. Whatever Rita wanted to do, I was going to be a part of."

Jesse Dansby, the pastor of Mt. Zion Baptist Church in Birmingham, spent the next few months preparing the six teenagers for what they might face at Woodlawn High. He gave them Scripture to read, including Psalm 37:1–9, which Cynthia read from her Bible every morning for strength:

Do not fret because of those who are evil or be envious of those who do wrong; for like the grass they will soon wither, like green plants they will soon die away.

Trust in the Lord and do good; dwell in the land and enjoy safe pasture.

Take delight in the Lord, and he will give you the desires of your heart.

Commit your way to the Lord; trust in him and he will do this:

He will make your righteous reward shine like the dawn, your vindication like the noonday sun.

Be still before the Lord and wait patiently for him; do not fret when people succeed in their ways, when they carry out their wicked schemes.

Refrain from anger and turn from wrath; do not fret—it leads only to evil.

For those who are evil will be destroyed, but those who hope in the Lord will inherit the land.

"He gave the Scripture to us to get our minds right and to prepare for what we were going to face," Holder said. "We had to be groomed to go. I think Reverend Dansby and our parents did a good job of letting us know what to expect and how to act."

She and the other African American students were aware they wouldn't be warmly greeted at their new school. Woodlawn High School was established in 1916 to educate the children of the white sales managers, engineers, and other executives who lived in the attractive Craftsman bungalows and Tudor Revival cottages in the booming Woodlawn Highlands neighborhood of East Birmingham.

The Woodlawn High School building, which was designed by architect Harry B. Wheelock and completed in January 1922, was more of a cathedral than a schoolhouse. The three-story brick building looked like a castle, complete with towers, Gothic arches, and tall spires shooting straight into the sky. The school's finely detailed auditorium even included a balcony. From 1934 to 1939, Sidney van Sheck and Richard Blauvelt Coe painted a large mural—seventy feet wide by eight feet tall—on the proscenium arch of the auditorium for the Works Progress Administration. The mural's inscription read: "Gloried Be They Who Foresaking Unjust Riches Strive in Fulfillment of Humble Tasks for Peace Culture and the Equality of All Mankind."

For nearly a half century, Woodlawn High School's doors were closed to African American students in America's most divided city.

However, there was nothing equal about Woodlawn High School. For nearly a half century, its doors were closed to African American students in America's most divided city. There were five all-white high schools in Birmingham—Ensley, Phillips, Ramsay,

West End, and Woodlawn. Until 1963, no black student had ever attended classes at any of the high schools.

There were three high schools for black students in Birmingham: Hayes, Parker, and Ullman. Parker High opened as the Negro High School in 1900, and after it was renamed in honor of its first principal, A. H. Parker, in 1946, it had an enrollment of 3,761 students, making it the country's largest all-black school. As the threat of federal desegregation loomed, Birmingham officials expanded Ullman High with a new three-story classroom wing in 1957, and then the new all-black Hayes High School opened on a seventeen-acre campus in 1960.

Not even federal court orders could break racial barriers in Alabama. On May 17, 1954, the U.S. Supreme Court struck down the separate but equal doctrine in American public schools in its historic *Brown v. Board of Education* decision. In an eleven-page opinion written by Chief Justice Earl Warren, the court firmly ruled: "We conclude that in the field of public education the doctrine of 'separate but equal' has no place. Separate educational facilities are inherently unequal."

But the *Brown v. Board of Education* decision fell on mostly deaf ears in Alabama, where segregation and Jim Crow laws were deeply embedded in the state's thick, red clay. In the 1950s, African Americans in Birmingham were still required to ride in the back of city buses, drink from "colored" water fountains, and use separate restrooms. Blacks weren't allowed to eat at downtown lunch counters and restaurants, and there were segregated movie theaters, department stores, parks, and swimming pools. Black high school football teams couldn't play at Legion Field, the "Old Gray Lady," which hosted University of Alabama games and was considered the football capital of the South.

Although 40 percent of Birmingham's population of nearly 350,000 residents in 1950 was black, the city had no African American police officers, firefighters, or elected officials. Only whites were hired as bus drivers, bank tellers, sales clerks, and cashiers in department stores. Black secretaries couldn't work for white businessmen, and white nurses weren't permitted to care for black patients, and vice versa. Even prison chain gangs were segregated—white inmates couldn't be shackled to black prisoners.

In 1950s Birmingham, black secretaries couldn't work for white businessmen, and white nurses weren't permitted to care for black patients, and vice versa.

Seven years after Jackie Robinson famously broke Major League Baseball's color barrier in 1947, and long after public schools in other regions of the country started opening their doors to black students, Birmingham was determined to keep its draconian Jim Crow laws intact no matter the cost. There were even city ordinances in place that made it unlawful for a "Negro and a white person to play together or in company with each other in any game of cards, dice, dominoes, checkers, baseball, softball, football, basketball or similar games." If blacks and whites couldn't play together, they certainly weren't allowed to learn together.

In 1969, African American Julius Clark was hired as an industrial arts teacher and boys' advisor at Woodlawn High. He had grown up in the Collegeville neighborhood in North Birmingham, one of the few areas reserved for black residents under the city's strict segregation laws. Clark attended all-black schools and his only interaction with white people occurred on the weekends or during the summers, when he went to nearby all-white neighborhoods to find domestic work. Clark spent many mornings cutting grass, raking leaves, and polishing floors for white families. He usually earned one dollar for four hours of work, which was enough money to pay for admission and concessions at an all-black movie theater. White women often gave him a sandwich and bottle of Coca-Cola for lunch.

"I rode behind the colored sign on the bus. I drank from the colored water fountain," Clark said. "I stepped off the sidewalk and onto the curb when the white ladies walked by. When I was old enough to register to vote, I paid the three-dollar poll tax and answered the crazy quizzes those people came up with. I followed the rules and regulations of the system."

The civil rights struggle occurred in two waves in Birmingham and each was met with much resistance and violence. After the *Brown v. Board of Education* decision, it took civil rights activists three long, conflict-ridden years to challenge Birmingham's segregation laws in schools. On August 20, 1957, Arthur Shores, one of the first and most successful African American attorneys in Alabama, petitioned the Birmingham Board of Education to admit thirteen black children from nine families to schools closest to their homes—all-white Graymont Elementary, Phillips High, and Woodlawn High. Shores, who attended segregated schools in Alabama as a child and then law school at the University of Kansas, became a civil rights pioneer after winning high-profile cases that had never before been litigated by black attorneys in the Deep South.

Despite Shores's growing reputation and successes, three African American families dropped their requests for transfers because of threats of violence. White supremacists weren't going to lie down. On Labor Day 1957, a group of Ku Klux Klansmen kidnapped a randomly chosen African American man while he was walking down a Birmingham road with his girlfriend. The six men took the mildly mentally disabled black man, J. Edward "Judge" Aaron, back to their Klan lair, where they beat and interrogated him. When the men were finished, they asked Aaron if he wanted to die or be castrated. Aaron chose to live, so the men mutilated him and left him in a creek bed, where he nearly bled to death before police found him. According to police, the men told Aaron it would happen to "any Negro sending his child to a white school." Birmingham police later arrested the suspects and charged them with mayhem. Two of the men turned state's witnesses, and the other four were convicted and sentenced to twenty years in prison. They were later pardoned by Alabama Governor George C. Wallace.

During a Birmingham Board of Education meeting that was attended by three Klansmen, the board tabled Shores's request to allow African American children to attend the schools closest to their homes. But Reverend Fred Shuttlesworth—who had filed a transfer petition on his two daughters' behalf—decided he wouldn't wait for a decision. Shuttlesworth's home had been bombed the previous Christmas Day, so he was well aware of the dangers of challenging segregationists. The bombing of Reverend Shuttlesworth's home wasn't an isolated incident. The Klan lighted so much dynamite in Birmingham during the 1950s and early 1960s that the city became known as "Bombingham." After Shuttlesworth's house was bombed, he emerged from the basement unscathed and led hundreds of African Americans onto buses in defiance of Jim Crow laws the next day.

On the morning of September 9, 1957, Shuttlesworth attempted to enroll his daughters, Patricia Ann and Ruby Fredericka, and two boys from their neighborhood—twelve-year-old Walter Wilson and seventeen-year-old Nathaniel Lee—at John Herbert Phillips High School. Two hours after the school day started, Reverend Shuttlesworth, his wife, Ruby, their bodyguard, and another civil rights activist drove the children to the school. A group of about twenty Klansmen was waiting for them at Phillips High, and the men attacked Shuttlesworth as he climbed out of the car. Other men tried to pull his wife, daughters, and the two boys from the car before police intervened. Reverend Shuttlesworth ran from the mob to divert the attackers' attention. He was knocked to the ground and beaten with brass knuckles, metal chains, and wooden clubs.

The reverend and his wife were treated for cuts and bruises at University Hospital. He vowed to try to enroll the students again the next morning. "Whether they kill us or not," he told *The Birmingham News*. Even though Shuttlesworth decided to postpone his plans for the next day, that didn't stop crowds of white segregationists from gathering outside Phillips High and other schools in anticipation of their return to their all-white schools.

When students arrived at Woodlawn High School on September 10, 1957, two hanging black effigies greeted them. Another one was hung that morning. Woodlawn High students boycotted classes in protest of possible integration, even though principal Ralph Martin threatened them with suspension. A handful of Woodlawn High students staged an impromptu demonstration at the school's flagpole, where they raised two Confederate flags.

Other students defiantly waved the Confederate Stars and Bars while chanting, "Two! Four! Six! Eight! We don't want to integrate!" *The Birmingham News* reported that assistant police chief J. C. Lance stopped two cars containing ten Woodlawn High students and confiscated a heavy club and a plastic-covered sack of firecrackers.

When students arrived at Woodlawn High School on September 10, 1957, two hanging black effigies greeted them.

"A number of students boycotted classes at Woodlawn High School this morning in protests against integration," *The Birmingham News* reported. "Youths demonstrated noisily on the school grounds and threw rocks at passing buses containing Negroes. They also jeered at passing automobiles containing Negroes."

A few days later, Shuttlesworth abandoned his plans and Birmingham's public schools remained segregated. It seemed the all-white schools would remain closed to African Americans forever. On January 14, 1963, newly elected Alabama governor Wallace delivered his infamous inauguration speech, in which he proclaimed, "In the name of the greatest people that have ever trod this earth, I draw the line in the dust and toss the gauntlet before the feet of tyranny, and I say segregation now, segregation tomorrow, segregation forever." Six months later, Wallace stood in a doorway of a building at the University of Alabama and blocked the entrance of two African American students trying to enroll at the school.

The summer of 1963 changed the course of history in Birmingham and the United States. Dr. Martin Luther King and other leaders of the Alabama Christian Movement for Human Rights and Southern Christian Leadership Conference led sit-ins at lunch counters and marches in the streets of Birmingham. King and other leaders were repeatedly jailed for their efforts. In a moment that would ultimately be a turning point in the civil rights movement, Birmingham public safety commissioner Eugene "Bull" Connor ordered his officers to turn their dogs and water hoses on thousands of student protesters during the Children's Crusade. Hundreds of young demonstrators were arrested and expelled from Birmingham schools, until federal courts intervened.

Finally, Birmingham School Board attorneys announced on August 30, 1963, that three schools—Graymont Elementary, Ramsay High, and West End High—would be desegregated. Demonstrators chanted and waved Confederate flags when eleven-year-old Dwight Armstrong and his ten-year-old brother, Floyd, attempted to enroll at Graymont Elementary on September 4, 1963. That night, attorney Arthur Shores's home was bombed for the second time in fifteen days and riots erupted in the streets. One man was shot dead and twenty-one others were injured. The next day, as President John F. Kennedy anguished over federal intervention in Birmingham, Wallace ordered the city to close the schools.

After a federal court order reopened the schools, the Armstrong brothers enrolled at Graymont Elementary on September 9, 1963. Richard Walker, another black student, enrolled at Ramsay High, and Patricia Marcus and Josephine Powell became the first black students at West End High. White students boycotted classes at West End High and assembled in the football field, where a student played a slow rendition of "Dixie" on a trumpet.

Six days later, an unthinkable act of terror changed Birmingham forever. A bomb exploded and killed four girls as they prepared for Sunday school at 16th Street Baptist Church. Three fourteen-year-old girls—Cynthia Wesley, Carole Robertson, and Addie Mae Collins—were killed, along with eleven-year-old Denise McNair. The four girls were targeted—along with everyone else attending the church—for one reason: the color of their skin.

Within days, the Federal Bureau of Investigation identified the prime suspects: Robert E. Chambliss, a well-known racist nicknamed "Dynamite Bob," and his fellow Klansmen Thomas E. Blanton, Herman Frank Cash, and Bobby Frank Cherry. They were members of the violent Eastview No. 13 Klavern, which met at Woodlawn's city hall in the 1960s. Chambliss was convicted of murder and sentenced to life in prison in 1977; but decades would pass before the other men faced criminal trials for their heinous crimes. Blanton and Cherry weren't convicted until nearly forty years after the bombing. Cash died in 1994 without ever being charged.

Nearly two years after the men bombed 16th Street Baptist Church, Cynthia Holder and the other African American students arrived at Woodlawn High for their first day. They were happy to see that the mobs of angry white segregationists, which greeted many black students at other newly integrated schools in the past, weren't there to meet them. A handful of Birmingham police officers stood guard outside the school, and the African American students were quickly ushered inside. Their plans to integrate Woodlawn High had largely been a secret. Only the students, their parents, and Reverend Dansby were aware of what they intended to do.

Time was slowly healing wounds in Birmingham, but racial

tension still simmered, especially in the Deep South. In March 1965, Martin Luther King led an estimated 25,000 protesters on a fifty-four-mile march from Selma, Alabama, to the state capitol building in Montgomery to show support for African American voting rights. Three weeks before Cynthia and the others enrolled at Woodlawn, a six-day race riot erupted in the Watts neighborhood of Los Angeles and resulted in thirty-four deaths, more than one thousand injuries, over three thousand arrests, and more than $40 million in property damage.

Somehow, the historic dismantling of Woodlawn High's color barrier went largely unnoticed in Birmingham, or at least outside of the school.

"It was very low-key and not much publicity was made of it when we went," Cynthia Holder said. "Our parents tried to keep it a secret. When we got to the school, we had to climb the big front steps. My parents told me to look straight forward and keep moving, and that's what I did."

The Birmingham News reported that afternoon that the new school year was off to a quiet start. According to the newspaper, fifty-three African American students had been approved for transfers to Birmingham's predominately all-white schools. Along with the six black students who started classes at Woodlawn High, eleven enrolled at Ensley High, nine at Phillips High, thirteen at Ramsay High, and two at West End High, and twelve others who enrolled in lower grades.

"Birmingham schools opened for registration of an expected 70,000 students today, beginning the third year of integrated operation without incident," the newspaper reported.

Dr. Theo Wright, the superintendent of the Birmingham Board of Education, told *The Birmingham News*, "We're very happy that everything is orderly. There were no incidents and the children who were approved for entrance were enrolled and there was no trouble anywhere."

Cynthia Holder and the other African American students weren't the only ones starting their first day at Woodlawn High. Tandy Gerelds, a newly hired science teacher and assistant football coach, was also beginning a new stage of his life. Gerelds was very familiar with Woodlawn High; he'd graduated from the school only five years earlier. A popular student and athlete, Gerelds was returning to teach at his alma mater only a few months after graduating from Auburn University. The young newlywed was anxious about starting his teaching and coaching career in the community that was home for most of his life.

It wouldn't take Gerelds long to realize he wasn't returning to the same school he'd left.

CHAPTER TWO

INTEGRATION

After nearly a half century of segregation, black students finally started attending Woodlawn High School in Birmingham, Alabama, in 1965. But Cynthia Holder and the other five African American pioneers were not truly a part of the predominantly white student body. They were ostracized and isolated by the majority of their classmates.

Once inside Woodlawn High, Cynthia and the others spent the first few periods of their first school day filling out registration forms and other paperwork. They took photographs for their student IDs. Each of the students was required to sign a "Declaration of Intention," which read, "Believing in the principles of co-operative government as necessary to intelligent citizenship and honorable character, I do hereby declare that if I am admitted as a student of this High School, I will support the constitution of the school to the best of my abilities."

After completing the paperwork, the students were given their class schedules. Cynthia Holder, Rita King, Myrtice Chamblin, and Leon Humphries were enrolled as juniors. Cedric King was a freshman, and Lily Humphries was a sophomore. For whatever reason, the administration separated the black juniors, and they never attended a class together during their two years at

Woodlawn High. They were required to face whatever lay ahead of them on their own.

For whatever reason, the administration separated
the black juniors; they were required to face
whatever lay ahead of them on their own.

Inside the classrooms, white students threw spitballs and chewing gum at Cynthia and the others. In the hallways between classes, white students often bumped into them or pushed them. They were cursed and called racial epithets. As soon as the bell rang to mark the end of a period, Cynthia and the other black students tried to find each other in the hallways so they could walk together to their next classes. In the lunchroom, one white boy liked to pour milk on the black students' heads. "Want to be white?" he asked them.

"It was very, very unnerving," Holder said. "The next year, it got a little bit better because Leon had an encounter with some boys, and he let them know that he wasn't going to take it. It got to where they weren't throwing spitballs or chewing gum anymore. There were a couple of teachers who were nice to us, but there also were some teachers who let us know that they weren't there to help us."

At least a few white students tried to help. Dr. Cary Speaker, who retired in May 2015 as pastor of Mountain Brook Presbyterian Church in Birmingham, was a junior at Woodlawn High when Cynthia and the other black students integrated the school. He had a study hall with Leon Humphries, and remembers other white students pelting him with spitballs on the first day. After witnessing what happened, Speaker moved to the chair directly behind Humphries. The students fired spitballs at him instead.

"I remember giving them what I thought was a dirty look," Speaker said. "I don't think I intimidated anyone."

The next spring, Woodlawn canceled its junior-senior prom because it would have to be integrated. The school's social sororities decided to have their own spring dance, and the female members sent out invitations to every student except the African Americans. Speaker, who was a wide receiver and safety on the football team, went to principal Elmer Eugene Moree's office to voice his concern.

"Do you know what's going on?" Speaker asked Moree.

"Of course I do," Moree said.

"You don't have a problem with it?" Speaker asked.

"Would you want your date dancing with a black boy?" Moree said.

"Well, I would think that would be up to her," Speaker said.

Speaker and three of his friends boycotted the dance and went on a canoe trip instead.

Getting home from Woodlawn High was often the most stressful time of the day for Cynthia and the others. On most days, Cynthia's father, Thomas Holder, who worked at the National Steel plant in Birmingham, picked her up from school. But on some days, Cynthia and her friends took the school bus home. Bus routes didn't extend to her all-black neighborhood of Zion City, which was located between West Boulevard and the airport, so Cynthia and her friends got off at a nearby stop, and then walked through an all-white neighborhood to get home.

"We didn't like to wait for my dad," Holder said. "If he wasn't there when the school day ended, we jumped on the first bus because we didn't want to have to wait in the bus line. I hated walking home. White kids would harass us, and we were always looking around to see if more kids were coming."

Somehow, Cynthia and the others survived. In June 1967, Cynthia, Rita King, Leon Humphries, and Myrtice Chamblin were among the first African Americans to graduate from Woodlawn High. Three other African American seniors—Delores Ambers, Carolyn Powe, and Webster Ware—enrolled at Woodlawn at the beginning of the 1966–67 school year, along with another eight black underclassmen. They defied great odds and graduated, despite facing enormous obstacles at the school.

"My shame about it fifty years later is that I wasn't brave enough to do anything more about it," Speaker said. "I grew up as a racist like any other white kid in Birmingham at the time. I knew it wasn't right, but I wasn't brave enough to do anything about it."

In the late 1960s, few opportunities were available for black students to become part of the student body. Woodlawn High's football team wasn't integrated until 1970; the sports teams and other extracurricular clubs were largely reserved for white students. The goal for African American students like Cynthia and the others was to get through the school day, stay out of trouble, and do well in their studies.

"It was a very cold shoulder," said Hank Erwin, who served as chaplain of Woodlawn High's football team in 1973 and 1974. "Integration was forced on the black community as well as the white community. The black kids were forcibly bused to the white schools to satisfy integration. The football team was the last bastion of white control. They couldn't keep the black children out of school, but they could keep them off the football team. They couldn't keep them from trying out, but they could make it very difficult for them to stay. It really took defiance and determination for the black kids to stay on the team."

Finally in 1970, five black players joined the school's B-team football squad, which was coached by Tandy Gerelds. The Colonels had an all-white varsity team until the following year, when Coach Gerelds became head coach. Five African American players—Jimmy Daniels, Rod Grigsby, Rickey Jones, Gary Speers, and Steven Washington—made the roster in 1971.

After Gerelds was named the school's head football coach in 1971, he had a difficult time persuading the best black athletes to try out for the team. At some point, Gerelds asked Julius Clark, the African American who worked as the assistant boys' advisor, for guidance on how to get more black students to play football. Clark's solution was simple.

"If you set something up for them to eat after practice, they'll come out for football," Clark told him. "What they're doing right after school is hurrying home so they can make sure they get their dinner. If they don't get home, they won't have anything to eat. Their brothers and sisters will eat everything."

Gerelds arranged for Woodlawn High's booster club to provide post-practice meals. Not long after, there were a growing number of black players on the varsity, B-team, and freshman squads, including a promising freshman defensive back named Tony Nathan.

"I remember going out for freshman football," said white player Denny Ragland, a ninth-grade quarterback in 1971. "We were all pretty wide-eyed and probably scared to death because we didn't know what we were getting into. It was my introduction to African Americans playing sports. I had been a pretty good athlete and did pretty well in grammar school with white guys; but when I was introduced to African Americans, I figured out there was a whole new dimension to sports."

Woodlawn High's first African American football players faced staggering odds. They not only had to fight to earn acceptance from their largely white teammates, but also their own communities. African American classmates criticized Rickey Jones and Steven Washington for playing what had been a white-only sport, and they were sometimes pelted with sticks and rocks by black neighbors while walking home from school.

"They were ostracized by their own people," said Reginald Greene, an African American lineman at Woodlawn High from 1971 to 1974. "They called them traitors."

"[The African American students] were ostracized by their own people," said Reginald Greene. "They called them traitors."

In the early 1970s, there weren't many other extracurricular opportunities for black students at Woodlawn High, so it was difficult for them to find their place in the student body. In 1971, the Tri-Hi-Y Club, a Christian service organization, had forty female members—thirty-nine whites and one black. The National Honor Society, comprised of juniors and seniors, had five white boys, seven white girls, and no African Americans. The National Junior Honor Society for sophomores was also an exclusively white club.

The school's marching band had about a half dozen black members, but the majorettes and flag corps didn't include any African American females. The Warblers, the popular men's choral group, had five blacks among fifty-two singers, and the women's Glee Club had three blacks among sixty-six performers. Vocational clubs such as Future Nurses, Future Teachers of America, and the Home Economics Club were more integrated, and the French and Spanish clubs, which had African American teachers as sponsors, also were more open to black students.

Six years after Cynthia Holder and the other pioneer black students first walked through the door, Woodlawn High was still segregated in most areas, even though more African Americans were attending the school. Tension between black and white students continued to mount, so in 1971 school administrators formed a race relations board made up of students and faculty. But that didn't help much, and the school's environment only became more toxic and dangerous.

"It wasn't about color," Julius Clark said. "It was about pride. When the school districts were redrawn, they transferred white kids to Woodlawn High. They transferred seniors from Banks High to Woodlawn High, and those kids had to start all over. Some of the white kids had never interacted with black people in a social setting. They didn't know how to adjust."

It didn't help that there was constant turnover in the school's administration. Principal Moree was a World War II veteran whose right leg had been broken by shrapnel in Northern Italy in October 1944. After Moree was injured, he was carried out of the Apennine Mountains on a stretcher by a mule, then a jeep, and then an ambulance. Moree, who spent more than a year at an Italian hospital and received the Purple Heart for his injuries, attended Howard College (now Samford University) in Birmingham and then the University of Alabama. He was a basketball coach at St. Clair County High School in Alabama, and then boys' advisor at Banks High and principal at Robinson Elementary School before taking over Woodlawn High.

In 1972, Moree left Woodlawn to become headmaster at Franklin Academy, a private school in Birmingham. B.B. Storie, a former Woodlawn High assistant football coach and head coach at Ensley High, replaced him and lasted only one year. Homer Wesley, who had two sons attending Woodlawn, was named the school's new principal in the summer of 1973.

In the late 1960s and early 1970s, it didn't take much to set off a disturbance at Woodlawn High. During the 1971–72 school year, a group of African American students asked administrators for permission to organize Black History Week, which Wesley granted. The week culminated with a program for the entire student body in the school's auditorium. As an African American girl recited a poem, the bell rang signaling the end of the period. A group of white students rose from their seats and left. Some of the black students felt they were disrespected, and a large argument ensued with pushing and shoving.

Rickey Jones, who was now a linebacker on the football team, jumped onstage and grabbed a microphone. He tried to calm everyone down before a melee broke out. Many of Jones's fellow African American students chastised him for trying to make peace, calling him an "Uncle Tom."

In the early 1970s, African American students started to fight back against oppression and became well organized in their efforts. While Reginald Greene was eating lunch in the cafeteria as a freshman in 1971, Steven Thomas, one of the leaders of the African American students, came running into the lunchroom with a handful of other black students. They went to where the black students were sitting and started pounding their fists on the tables.

They screamed, "Get up! Get up!" The black students marched to the football field, where Thomas read a list of grievances that African American students wanted the administration to address. Gerelds came to the stadium and saw Greene standing in the mob. Gerelds pointed at Greene and motioned for him to come over.

"I don't want my players caught up in that mess," Gerelds told him. "You go back to class."

Gerelds had a simple rule for his football players: if a fight broke out in a classroom, they were supposed to leave their class and go to the gymnasium.

Gerelds had a simple rule for his football players: if a fight broke out in a classroom, they were supposed to leave their class and go to the gymnasium.

"Our players could not be involved in it, no matter what their feelings were," said Jerry Stearns, the team's defensive coordinator and a physical education teacher. "It could have ruined our entire team."

While some of the incidents at Woodlawn High were simply misunderstandings between teenagers, others were violent, racial attacks. Julius Clark remembers the mother of a student calling the front office one day to ask if her son had arrived at school. When she was told her son was walking through the front door, she told Clark to keep him in the front office until she arrived there. When the mother walked into the office, she told her son, "Give it to me, now!" The boy, an African American, pulled a sawed-off shotgun out from under his trench coat and turned it over to his mother.

During one of the worst incidents in the fall of 1972, a fight broke out between white and black students on the front steps of the boys' gymnasium. Roderick Walls, an African American student and now an attorney in Birmingham, remembers a fight between black and white students on the football field during his PE class. Two days later, when Walls and his black classmates tried to enter the gym, a mob of white students blocked the doors. Another fight broke out on the steps, and the violence quickly spread to other parts of the school. Making matters worse, a few of the white students often wore bicycle or motorcycle chains as belts. When fights broke out, they'd wrapped the belts around their fists as weapons. On this day, as the white students hurled their belts during the fight, some of the black students used two-by-fours from a construction site to defend themselves. A few students were seriously injured before teachers and coaches broke up the melee.

"My sister was in a classroom inside the school, and she saw a lot of blood when she left," Walls said.

After that particular fight, the Birmingham Board of Education made the decision to close Woodlawn High for a few days to allow tempers to cool off. Birmingham police officers monitored the hallways when students returned to classes the next week.

"It was ugly," said Walls, who graduated from Woodlawn High in 1975 and attended law school at the University of Alabama. "It was unnecessary. Woodlawn was tough and there always seemed to be tension. Sometimes, I wonder how I survived."

Students weren't the only ones causing problems at Woodlawn High. At least one African American former student who was dismissed for disciplinary problems sometimes waited in the parking lot to cause trouble after school. As football players Bubba Holland and Kirk Price made their way to Holland's green Volkswagen Bug after practice one day, the former student, who was popularly known as "Ikner," and four other black students attacked them as they climbed into the car. Ikner believed Price was harassing a younger black student, and Ikner was going to make him pay.

Price was sitting in the passenger seat, and Ikner reached through the open window with a knife. Price tried to cover his face to protect himself, but he was trapped in the small car and could barely move. He suffered several cuts on his arms and hands. Holland tried to reach across the car to roll up the window, but another man reached into his side of the car and started pummeling him.

As Ikner began to make his way to the other side of the car, Price reached into the backseat and grabbed a shotgun off the floorboard. He drew the gun back as far as he could and rammed the butt of it into the face of the man attacking Holland. The blow knocked the man back, but Ikner, who had made it around the car to the open window, now had control of the gun. Ikner shattered a window and pumped the shotgun. He quickly took aim and pulled the trigger. The next thing Holland and Price heard was, "Click!"

The shotgun wasn't loaded. Thankful to be alive, Price burst out of the car and rushed the group of attackers. Holland ran toward the athletic complex to find help. Price was left to fend off five would-be assailants, who had him cornered in the street. Ikner picked up a stop sign, which was lying nearby on the ground and swung it at Price's knees, knocking him to the ground. The mob jumped on Price, repeatedly kicking and punching him. Badly injured, Price heard shouting. His teammates were running from the school to save him. As Holland, Peyton Zarzour, Bobby

Thompson, and a couple of other players ran toward Price, Ikner and his friends fled.

As the situation at Woodlawn High became more violent, students weren't the only targets of people who wanted to do harm. As Gerelds left the lunchroom on the first floor of the school one afternoon, he was surrounded by an angry group of black students. The crowd backed him into a corner near the stairwell. Frantically looking for help, Gerelds saw a black teacher coming down the stairs. When black students initially enrolled at Woodlawn, a few African-American teachers were transferred to the school to help ease their transition. For whatever reason, the teacher turned around and left without saying anything.

At that point, Gerelds realized there was no way out. Suddenly, Gerelds heard the familiar and thunderous voice of a friend. Clark, the African American assistant boys' advisor, heard the commotion while sitting in his office down the hall. He muscled his way through the mob and stood between Gerelds and his would-be attackers. "You're going to have to hurt me if you want to hurt him," Clark told the students. Instead of taking on Clark and Gerelds, the crowd dispersed.

"Tandy always gave me credit for saving his life," Clark said, "but I've always tried to figure out what I did to save it. We were really close. The thing that really knitted us together was our religious beliefs."

Over the next two years, Gerelds's faith would be tested myriad times as he tried to build an integrated football team at Woodlawn High. White students didn't like or trust the black players, and the black players didn't like or trust the white players—or their white coaches. Gerelds knew the distrust wasn't a recipe for success. Somehow, Gerelds had to find a way to make it work.

CHAPTER THREE

THE COACH

While Tandy Gerelds was still a student at Woodlawn High, he injured his right shoulder at football practice. Since he was also on the baseball team, he taught himself to throw left-handed until his injured shoulder healed. He would catch balls in the outfield with a glove on his left hand. Then he'd remove the glove and throw the ball left-handed. Undersized compared to most of his classmates, Gerelds knew he had to become a scrappy player and an overachiever to succeed. From an early age, Gerelds never wanted anyone to outwork him. He carried that same mind-set into coaching, often telling his players, "There are going to be times when the people you are competing against are more physically gifted than you are. You can't control that. But what you can control is your own preparation. If you outwork them, sometimes it doesn't matter if they're more talented. Through hard work, discipline, and execution you can and will beat superior talent. Don't let the thing you have control over be the thing that beats you. Always outwork your competition."

Thomas Tandy Gerelds grew up on the East Side of Birmingham. He was a multisport athlete, and was a part of winning teams from an early age. His Little League baseball teams at Wahouma Park were always competing at a high level. His American Legion Pony League team played in a national tournament. Gerelds played football and baseball at Woodlawn High School and was talented enough to letter multiple years in both sports. During Gerelds's freshman season in 1956, the Colonels went 10–0 in football under Coach Kenny Morgan. That season, Woodlawn shut out seven opponents and outscored its competition 219–26 in 10 games. The Colonels slipped to 5–4 in Gerelds's sophomore season and then went 7–2–1 when he was a junior. During his senior season in 1959, the Colonels finished 5–5 under first-year coach Johnny Howell.

Gerelds wasn't the most physically gifted athlete, and he certainly wasn't the biggest player on the football field or baseball diamond. Gerelds was strong and quick, but he was only five-foot-eight. It didn't take his coaches long to figure out they would have a difficult time finding anyone who was more competitive. Gerelds could really hit a baseball, and he was tough and wasn't afraid to make a tackle in football.

Gerelds did have a very strong arm, and his all-around baseball skills were good enough to draw the attention of scouts from Major League Baseball teams, including the New York Yankees. His dreams of playing in the major leagues came to an end, however, after he was hurt during spring football practice in 1958. While playing running back, Gerelds attempted to score a touchdown by diving over the top. Someone clipped his feet, sending him headfirst into the ground. Gerelds extended his arm to break his fall and badly injured his shoulder. Even though his shoulder got stronger, he ultimately needed surgery to repair it, and his arm was never the same.

Even with an injured throwing arm, Gerelds was able to finish his baseball career at Woodlawn High. In 1960, he enrolled at

Auburn University. He worked busing tables in the athletic dorm cafeteria and joined the baseball team as a nonscholarship player. As a sophomore in 1962, Gerelds hit .222 in nine at-bats for the Tigers. The next season, after new coach Paul Nix awarded Gerelds a scholarship, he hit .270 with six RBIs, helping Auburn finish 17–8 and win a Southeastern Conference championship. The Tigers played in an NCAA District 3 Tournament in Gastonia, North Carolina, losing to West Virginia 2–1 and Florida State 4–3. As a senior in 1964, Gerelds was one of Auburn's best players, hitting .303 with one home run and 23 RBIs.

But Gerelds's hitting record wasn't the most significant event in his life in 1964. That year, he met an Auburn freshman, Debbie Johnson, who would soon become his wife. Debbie first noticed Tandy when she was a fourteen-year-old freshman at Woodlawn High. She was the youngest girl in her class because she'd skipped a grade in grammar school. She was a cheerleader and was spunky, outgoing, and strong-willed. Her best friends were Tandy's sister Marsha and his cousin Patsy Emerson. During a sleepover for the Sigma Tau Sorority at the Gereldses' house, Debbie noticed Marsha's older brother, who was a senior at Woodlawn. At Debbie's request, Marsha asked Tandy if he had any romantic interest in her friend. "That little Johnson girl?" Tandy said. "She's just a kid."

"That was it, and I never said a word about it the next four years," Debbie said.

Five years later, Tandy noticed Debbie on the Auburn campus during her freshman year in 1964. Debbie was dating another boy at the time, but when Patsy told her that Tandy had asked about that "little Johnson girl," she agreed to let him have her telephone number. Tandy called her a few days later and asked her out. Debbie was supposed to be going to a concert on campus with her current boyfriend, but she canceled (she told the boy she couldn't leave her dorm hall because she was being punished for participating in a water balloon fight) and went out with Tandy instead.

They skipped the concert out of fear that Debbie's boyfriend might be there, and instead went to a local ice cream drive-up that was something of an Auburn institution. The place was nicknamed "The Flush" because of its unfortunate actual name, Sani-Freeze. It was a popular hangout for students who needed a break from their studies. Debbie had a good time with Tandy, and then she broke the news to her current boyfriend a few days later—she'd met the man she was going to marry. Over the next few weeks, Tandy and Debbie spent as much time together as they could and then headed back to Birmingham for Christmas break.

When Debbie broke the news to her current boyfriend,
she said she'd met the man she was going to marry.

"It was one of those things where you just knew it was that person. But I didn't know how he felt," Debbie said, "so I had to play it cool."

Once back home, Tandy and Debbie visited with older friends, many of whom were already married. Tandy took a temporary job to make extra Christmas money, and Debbie spent a lot of time with her grandparents. Tandy had a habit of always acting immediately on what he believed—right then, in the moment. It could be a great thing, but it could also give way to seemingly rash decisions. This time, Tandy believed Debbie was the girl who was supposed to be with him forever. During one of their dates over the holidays, Tandy asked her, "Hey, I don't have to work on Christmas Eve. You want to get married?"

"Yes, I do," she said.

"I knew the first time I kissed him that he was the one for me," Debbie said. "I felt it in my heart."

More than anything, Debbie wanted a normal family life. She'd grown up in a dysfunctional home: her father was an alcoholic and was abusive to her mother, who abused painkillers. Police were called to Debbie's home a lot, but her mother refused to throw her father out. On many nights, Debbie lay in her bed awake, praying that her father wouldn't come home drunk. When Debbie's father was sober, she enjoyed being around him. They listened to baseball games and horse races together on the radio. But most of the time, she stayed in her room to avoid him when he was drinking.

"I thought if I was really smart, my daddy would quit drinking," Debbie said. "I thought if I made the cheerleading squad, my daddy would quit. I thought if I was elected to the student council, he'd quit. But no matter what I did, he couldn't quit drinking."

Debbie's parents were married for fifteen years until her mother finally had enough. She filed for divorce and moved to California. Debbie's grandparents bought her parents' home, and Debbie decided to live with her grandparents so she could stay at Woodlawn High School. Her best friend, Diane Massey, lived across the street, and the Masseys' home had often been a refuge for Debbie when her father was drunk or her parents were fighting. Debbie's aunt and uncle lived down the street.

Debbie's grandfather Otis Hammett was a coal miner, and her grandmother Ruby was a homemaker. Her grandparents were strict and old-fashioned, but they loved her dearly and provided her with a stable home. Debbie attended church with them at 66th Street Baptist Church in Birmingham, where she invited the Lord into her heart when she was twelve years old. She still remembers the church hymn "Holy, Holy, Holy" playing as she accepted the invitation to become a Christian and walked to the altar with her heart pounding.

On Christmas Eve 1964, Tandy and Debbie drove across the state line to Trenton, Georgia, where they were married in a courthouse. Their friends Judy and Dan Hunt went with them and served as witnesses. Tandy wore a green corduroy suit; Debbie wore a white wool outfit and a tiny hat with a veil. When Tandy told his parents that he was getting hitched, his mother gave him a package of new underwear.

Once Tandy and Debbie arrived at the courthouse, they filled out the required paperwork and were sent to a lab for blood tests. Tandy noticed that most of the women in the lab were expecting. He said loud enough for everyone else to hear, "She's not pregnant! She's not pregnant!" When it was their turn to exchange vows, the judge joked with Debbie: "Did you have to hunt long to find him?" implying that she was out of Tandy's league and could have done better. Tandy was twenty-two; Debbie was eighteen. A few weeks later, they realized they could have been married in Alabama, where the state age requirement was eighteen years. In hindsight, Debbie remembered, "It was more exciting to go across state lines to get married."

After returning to Birmingham, Tandy called his mother and told her he was officially married. His mother told him that they had allowed his younger sister to open Christmas presents without him there. Then she asked if he and Debbie wanted to come over and play board games with them. Tandy and his new wife were spending their wedding night at the Birmingham Motel on Highway 278, so he told his mother they'd see them on Christmas morning.

After the holidays, the couple returned to Auburn, where Tandy finished his bachelor's degree in education. When it was time to start searching for a job, Tandy initially thought he might go into sporting goods sales. But then he settled on teaching and coaching. As luck would have it, Woodlawn High School had an opening for an assistant football coach and science teacher. He applied for the job, aced the interview, and was offered the position. After Tandy graduated from Auburn in May 1965, he and Debbie returned to Birmingham, and he went to work at his alma mater. Tandy knew he'd received a big break. He was starting his coaching career at one of the top high school programs in Alabama and would be working for John Lee Armstrong, an up-and-coming coach.

Armstrong, who'd played baseball and football at Howard College in Birmingham, was about to begin his first season as a head coach. Tandy set out to become the best coach he could be by learning as much as he could from Armstrong, and he and Debbie settled into married life. At times, it was a little bit awkward for her because the seniors on Tandy's football team were only two years younger than she was. Many of them were her close friends when she was still attending Woodlawn.

"Do you want us to call you Debbie or Mrs. Gerelds?" the players asked her.

"I don't know," she told them. "Let me ask Tandy."

Led by halfback Larry Helms, the Colonels started the 1965 season with a 3–0–1 record and were ranked as high as No. 8 in the state in Class 4A. But then the Colonels lost four of their last five games, including a disappointing 20–14 defeat against rival Banks High School at Legion Field. After Armstrong's first season at Woodlawn High, he surprisingly left to become head coach at Howard College, which by then had changed its name to Samford University. Tandy worried that Woodlawn's new coach wouldn't keep him as an assistant. Debbie was expecting their first child, and he didn't want to be looking for a job.

Woodlawn High officials hired Bill Burgess, the assistant coach of their rival Banks High, to replace Armstrong, and Burgess agreed to keep Tandy on his staff. Burgess was a Birmingham native; he'd attended Jones Valley High School and played fullback and linebacker at Auburn. Tandy was grateful that Burgess kept him on staff. Debbie gave birth to Jessica Tandy Gerelds on May 17, 1966; their son, Todd, was born two years later and then a daughter, Jill, in 1972.

Coach Burgess and his wife, Gaynell, taught Tandy and Debbie about the importance of family. In the coaching profession, Burgess told them, your loved ones might be your only supporters when things aren't going well. Tandy liked to joke that most people don't have critics watching their work from bleacher seats every week. He knew that his coaching decisions and the product he put on the field were going to be scrutinized and that he would ultimately be judged by the games' outcomes.

Burgess created a true family atmosphere among the coaches, their wives, and children. Families attended practices and games together. In fact, coaches' wives and players' parents volunteered to pick up Debbie and her kids during the first few seasons because she still hadn't learned to drive. The coaches' families spent time together after games to eat, laugh, and enjoy one another.

Bill Burgess and his wife, Gaynell, taught Tandy and Debbie about the importance of family.

With the coaches spending so much time at school, the wives ran the houses. They bathed and dressed the kids, loaded them in cars, and then drove them to the stadium to watch games. The routine was the same every week, and it wasn't always easy. The wives and children sat in the bleachers and listened to people who didn't know anything about football criticize their husbands and fathers. The families were there for each other and helped one another manage the craziness. Debbie and Tandy would learn that the friendships forged through such times of stress, fun, frustration, and growth were the kind that lasted forever. Football season meant long hours of work and stress at school for their husbands. With their husbands spending so much time at school and on the practice field, the wives bonded together to support each other.

Burgess's tenure had a rocky start, as the Colonels went 3–6 in 1966 and 1–7–1 in 1967, with their lone victory in his second season coming against Phillips High School 14–12 at Legion Field. The next season, Woodlawn performed a little bit better, finishing 3–6. Even though the first few seasons were frustrating under Coach Burgess, the Colonels were well positioned to have a competitive team in 1969.

Colonels halfback David Langner and his brother Scott were both going to be seniors, along with Greg Gantt, who was one of the best kickers and punters in the state. The Colonels won their first eight games in 1969, scoring 40 points or more in five contests. After beating Ensley High 17–7 at Legion Field on November 7, Woodlawn was undefeated and ranked No. 5 in Class 4A going into its regular season finale against rival Banks High. The Colonels defeated the Jets 28–20 at Legion Field and finished the regular season with a perfect 10–0 record. They played Lee High School of Montgomery in the first round of the state playoffs, falling 28–13 at the Cramton Bowl. It was a disappointing finish, but there was little doubt the Colonels had finally turned the corner after a string of mediocre seasons.

After the Colonels finished 4–6 in 1970, Coach Burgess resigned to become head coach at Oxford High School in Oxford, Alabama. Over the next 14 seasons, the Yellow Jackets went 106–42–1 and reached the playoffs eight times. In 1985, Burgess was named the head coach at Jacksonville State University in Jacksonville, Alabama, which competed at the NCAA Division II level. In 1992, he led the Gamecocks to a Division II national championship. He and Gerelds remained close friends over the years.

After six seasons as an assistant coach at Woodlawn High, Gerelds was elevated to head coach before the 1971 season. He had proven to be a more than capable leader while coaching Woodlawn's B-teams. He guided the Colonels to three city B-team championships and a four-year record of 26–4–1. He also coached the school's baseball team (one of his pitchers was Doyle Alexander, who went on to win 194 games in 19 seasons in the major leagues) and worked with all other sports except track. City schools leaders overwhelmingly endorsed his hiring.

"We are extremely pleased to have as fine a coach as Coach Gerelds already on the Woodlawn staff and in a position to take over the head coaching duties," city schools athletics director Bill Harris told *The Birmingham News*. "Coach Gerelds is a fine young coach. He is a very hard worker, and a head-coaching job is what he's been working for. He is well liked by the athletes at Woodlawn and by the people in the Woodlawn community, and we know he will do an outstanding job."

Burgess also endorsed the promotion of his former assistant and good friend.

"I hated to leave Woodlawn," Burgess told the *News*. "But I'm happy that it provided the opportunity for Tandy to move up. We have worked closely together here, and I can't think of a better person to fill the position. Much of any success we might have had at Woodlawn can be directly attributed to the work of Coach Gerelds and the other assistants here. I have all the confidence in the world in Tandy's ability, and I feel very strongly that he will give Woodlawn an athletic program that the school and the community can be proud of."

One of Gerelds's first decisions as head coach was hiring Jimmy Williams, an assistant football coach and track coach at Phillips High School. Assistants Jerry Stearns and Jim Price would soon join his staff as well.

"We have some good kids here at Woodlawn, and I hope we can continue to give Woodlawn students and fans the type of program they have become accustomed to during Coach Burgess' time here," Gerelds told the *News*. "We hope to continue the program Coach Burgess has built, and anything we do here will be due to a great extent to the groundwork Coach Burgess did when Woodlawn football was at a low point."

In his first season, Gerelds would have to replace the nucleus of his team's high-powered offense. The Colonels had to replace four seniors who left to play for Southeastern Conference schools—fullback Rick Harbuck (Auburn), quarterback Bobby Parks (Mississippi State), end Rick Meadows (Alabama), and end Gordon Robbins (Georgia). With much of his firepower gone, Gerelds knew he would have to change the way the Colonels were going to play on offense. Instead of being a pass-happy team, Woodlawn would have to beat opponents with toughness and a strong running game.

Instead of being a pass-happy team, Woodlawn would have to beat opponents with toughness and a strong running game.

"We're going to have to run the football," Gerelds told *The Birmingham News* shortly before the 1971 season. "We can't expect to start out with the passing game we ended up with last year, because it was a mighty fine one. We really don't know what we'll have right now. But we've got some good kids and it's really up to them. They've got a hard job ahead of them. But if it can be done, they're the type of kids who can do it. Certainly, we'll be trying to improve the 4–6 record of last year. On paper, we're not as good, but I believe our attitude will be much better."

Gerelds also wasn't sure what to expect from his defense, even with top tacklers Bubba Holland and Kirk Price coming back. Jerry Stearns joined his staff shortly after graduating from Livingston State College in Livingston, Alabama. Stearns didn't have any coaching experience, but he was recommended by one of

Gerelds's close friends. Shortly after hiring him, Gerelds brought Stearns into his office and put him in front of the chalkboard.

"I'm going to draw an offense on the board, and I want you to draw up a 50 defense and any adjustments you would make," Gerelds said.

Stearns looked at Gerelds like he was speaking French, not knowing that a 50 defense was an alignment with five defensive linemen and two linebackers behind them.

"When I graduated from school, I thought I knew a lot about football," Stearns said. "I couldn't even draw up a 50 defense. I'd heard of it, but I didn't know anything more than who I was supposed to block when I was playing in college. I didn't know anything about where the secondary was or where the linebackers were supposed to go. It really embarrassed me that I couldn't even draw up a 50 defense."

While other coaches might have fired Stearns on the spot, Gerelds encouraged him and told him they'd learn together.

Instead of firing Stearns on the spot, Gerelds encouraged him and told him they'd learn together.

"From that point forward, I was bound and determined that it would never happen again," Stearns said. "I read every book I could get my hands on, talked to a lot of people, and watched a lot of football."

Eventually, Gerelds trusted Stearns enough to turn his entire defense over to him. Gerelds's coaching philosophy was simple: limit the game plan so the players could run a select number of plays to perfection. On offense, the Colonels ran a Wing-T offense, which was very popular at the time. Eventually, they would switch to an I-formation, which was similar to the offense the University of Southern California was running.

"Every play and situation that you have in the Wing-T offense is directly related to the belly series on the weak side and the buck series on the strong side," Gerelds wrote before his death. He went on to say:

> Before you can venture out of these two series, you have to know that every player who will ever play has a good, almost perfect understanding of these two basic plays. The third-string guard has to know these two basic plays, as well as the first-string guard. You have to know that when everything else is uncertain, these two plays can be run effectively by everyone. You have to always plan everything you do as if the starters are all hurt and you have to rely on the subs. If you do this, when a few get hurt, you will not digress. Players do not always have to be great athletes, and they won't be, but they have to know what to do all the time.

Gerelds also wanted his team to be one of the most well-conditioned squads in the state. It didn't make him the most popular coach among his players, but it enabled his teams to fight through fatigue in the fourth quarter, when the outcome of many games would still be in doubt.

"Consistency and endurance are the key to any great program," Gerelds wrote. He continued:

> Any team can have spurts of greatness. Any team can make a run or build some momentum. Only great teams maintain momentum for

long periods of time. To get consistency, the most important facets of
a program have to be repeated until it is second nature to the team.
It has to be something they do like walking and talking. It can't be
something they doubt they can do; it is something they know they
can do. Endurance is achieved by working hard when you are tired.
It is developed gradually over a period of time.

Gerelds wanted his teams to be rough and tough, but he wasn't going to become a raging madman to make it happen. It wasn't his personality. During a moment of self-reflection, Gerelds promised himself he would be a positive coach, a mentor and leader who would make a lasting impact on his players.

Gerelds promised himself he would be a
positive coach, a mentor and leader who would
make a lasting impact on his players.

"You have to have an order of everything you do if it is going to work," Gerelds wrote. He went on to say:

Everyone has to follow the same rules and regulations. Everyone has
to feel like they are part of the program. Every player has to have a
status. It is better to have an identity that is low than to have no
identity at all. It is better to say little and do more than to say a lot
and do little. You cannot fool kids; they know when you are fair.
You have to tell the kids the truth and be fair. Everything that you
make kids do is important—it can affect their lives. Do a few things
excellent, not a lot of things good. God put everyone on earth with

a winning spirit. Kids don't start out losers. Parents and environ-
ments dictate the track a young person takes. Everyone would like to
feel special and needed. Team sports give a group of young people the
feeling of being special that they ordinarily wouldn't have.

From the very beginning of his career, Gerelds showed a lot
of promise as a head coach. The Colonels beat Western-Olin
High School 40–20 in his head coaching debut on September
10, 1971. Then they posted back-to-back 21–0 shutouts of
Vestavia Hills and Ramsay. Just like that, the Colonels were 3–0
and ranked No. 7 in the state in Class 4A. It couldn't be this easy,
could it? With tailbacks Lloyd Alford and Rick Pike running
the ball, and quarterback David O'Hare directing the Wing-T
offense, the Colonels looked like a well-oiled machine to start
the season.

But then the wheels started coming off. Woodlawn lost five
of its next six games, scoring seven points or less in four of the
contests. In a 27–0 loss to Phillips High School, the Colonels ran
for only 49 yards and passed for only 41 on four completions.
Woodlawn blew a 17–7 lead in the second half of a 28–17 loss to
Ensley. No matter what Gerelds did, he couldn't get his offense
turned around. Despite how hard he tried, he couldn't find an
answer.

Somehow, the Colonels ended the season with a 21–18 victory over Banks High, which helped erase a lot of the disappointment during Gerelds's first season. He'd led Woodlawn High to
a victory over its biggest rival, which carried a lot of weight with
the school's administration, alumni, and community leaders. The
Jets nearly came from behind to win, after freshman quarterback
Jeff Rutledge returned from an injured throwing shoulder to lead

two scoring drives in the second half. Rutledge's gutsy performance would be an omen of things to come in the rivalry.

After finishing his first season with a 5–5 record, Gerelds was
determined to become a better head coach. So much so that his
competitive drive and will to win consumed him over the next
couple of seasons. He later admitted to being overconsumed with
winning in a testimony that he wrote shortly before his death:

My decisions now affected many people. For the first time in my life,
I felt stress and pressure. The need for success and the drive to be the
very best completely engulfed my personality and changed my way
of living, both personally and professionally. Professionally, I cared
as much about success as I did the young men I was coaching. I be-
came obsessed with competition and winning. Nothing else seemed
to fulfill my wants or ego. I considered a defeat a personal flaw in
my armor.

I decided I wanted to be the very best coach, and I would push
myself, assistant coaches, and players until I reached my goal. At
the same time, I was teaching science. Unfortunately, I was not
interested in science or, for that matter, the students. However, I did
an adequate job of teaching, for fear that my principal or fellow
workers would think that I was not doing the job.

I worked about sixteen hours a day. Coaching became an obses-
sion with me. My success came slow, but steady, but not near enough
to satisfy my inward drive for personal success. I involved myself so
deeply in my job that I had very little time for my family or friends.
I know now that I was never going to fill the void in my life. I
thought it would be filled by winning football games. I did become
a good football coach. I learned my lessons from better coaches than
myself, who usually beat my team. I learned to be sound at what

you do and to have an order of football, or anything else for that
matter. I wanted to be well organized and became upset if anything
or anyone got out of order.

During the next three seasons, Gerelds would learn that he
wasn't really in control of anything. It would take the influence
of a reluctant superstar and two strangers to make him realize it.

CHAPTER FOUR

THE EVANGELIST

The first thing Woodlawn High School football coach Tandy Ge-relds noticed when Wales Goebel knocked on his office door in August 1973 was his height—and his bushy hair. Goebel was quite an imposing figure; the former college basketball player was six-foot-four. Gerelds guessed he might have been even a few inches taller because of his thick, wavy hair.

"Tandy said his hair nearly filled the entire doorway," said his wife, Debbie. "He never forgot his hair."

Gerelds, who was about to begin his third season as the Colonels' head coach and his first year as the school's assistant principal, didn't recognize Goebel.

"Who are you?" Gerelds asked.

"I'm Wales Goebel," Goebel told him, with a Southern drawl as thick as mayhaw jelly.

At the time, Gerelds couldn't have imagined the impact Goebel would ultimately have not only on his players' lives but also his own. Then again, Gerelds didn't know anything about Goebel.

For more than a decade, Goebel had been changing young people's lives across the state of Alabama. However, he had never encountered challenges like those he was about to walk into at

Woodlawn High, which had been ripped apart by racial tension following the government-mandated desegregation. Others warned Goebel about what was happening at Woodlawn High. He knew there was only one answer to the problems—Jesus Christ.

Goebel knew there was only one answer to the problems at Woodlawn High—Jesus Christ.

Wales Goebel was born in Tallapoosa, Georgia, which is about fifty miles west of Atlanta and sits in Haralson County on the Alabama border. He was the sixth oldest of eight sons. His father, A. G. Goebel, a German immigrant, remarried after his first wife died. Goebel's mother, the former U.Z. Jones, had three sons with his father and helped raise five boys from his first marriage. Wales's father owned a grocery store and meat market. Religion and faith were rarely discussed in their home.

"I grew up in a home that was not Christian," Goebel said. "My father was from Germany—the old country—and he was an atheist. He was a very hard man and a very stern German."

Goebel can only recall his family attending church one day every year. His mother took her sons to Christmas Eve services because churches in the area handed out fresh fruit. Most of his friends' families attended church every Sunday, and Goebel once asked his father why they didn't go more often.

"My dad had an old German word he liked—humbug," Goebel said. "Everything he disagreed with was humbug, and he thought religion was humbug."

When Goebel was seventeen, he became involved in the lucrative, yet illegal, business of bootlegging in Haralson County. The county was once home to a thriving wine industry before Prohibition in the 1920s, and then moonshine or corn mash became the county's most profitable export over the next couple of decades. Goebel and a close friend worked as taxi drivers in Tallapoosa, which they figured out was an effective cover for bootlegging. Before long, they were buying gallons of moonshine from distillers, bottling it into smaller quantities, and then selling the hooch out of their taxis. Goebel made a nice living for a teenager, until a friend warned him that Haralson County sheriff's deputies were aware of his illicit business.

"It was an easy thing to do at the time to make money," Goebel said. "You don't consider yourself doing something bad or crooked when you're a kid. When somebody says, 'Hey, Wales, we can make a little money doing this,' you don't think twice about it. But I was concerned that if I did get caught and went to jail, it would affect my mother greatly."

After his friend's warning, Goebel decided to get out of the moonshine business. Two nights after dumping what was left, he was pulled over by police, who searched his 1946 Ford Coupe. They didn't find any moonshine. Two of his best friends weren't so lucky and ended up serving time in federal prison.

After graduating from Haralson County High School in 1946, Goebel enlisted in the Navy and worked as a radio operator aboard ships. For two years, he served on boats that swept for mines up and down the East Coast following the end of World War II. Once Goebel was discharged from the Navy, he returned to Tallapoosa and enrolled at West Georgia College in nearby Carrollton.

Goebel played on the school's basketball team, along with his cousin Ivan "Buddy" Goebel, and was elected president of the student body. He started dating a girl, Jean Duff, and took her home to meet his mother. Goebel told his mother he wanted to marry Jean. But Goebel didn't believe Jean would accept his proposal because she was aware of the secret he was keeping from his mother—he was an alcoholic.

"I couldn't quit drinking," Goebel said. "It started to affect my ball playing, and they kicked me off the basketball team. The dean of students called me in and told me I was going to be expelled. Shortly thereafter, Jean gave me my walking papers."

At twenty-one years old, Goebel hit rock bottom. After he was expelled from college, he returned to live with his mother. It was then that he finally told her about his drinking problem. One of his good friends on West Georgia College's football team called him. He wanted Goebel to attend church with him the next Sunday.

"My buddy was always trying to encourage me to go to church with him," Goebel said. "It was the last place I wanted to be on Sunday mornings. But he was a good friend, and I knew he was different. I didn't know why he wanted to be involved with me."

Goebel's friend drove him to a Methodist church in La-Grange, Georgia. On the way, Goebel asked his friend to stop at the county line so he could buy a beer.

"Wales, you don't want a beer before you go to church," his friend said. "Let's get one on the way back."

When they arrived at the church, Goebel didn't want to go inside. But his friend persuaded him to walk through the doors, and they sat and listened to the preacher's sermon. The pastor was a student from Asbury College in Wilmore, Kentucky. A group of students from the college were traveling to churches across the

Southeast as part of their mission. At the end of the service, the preacher asked the congregation, "If you have a choice of going to heaven or hell, which one would you choose?" He gave his audience a few minutes to consider the question.

"Some of you have said you would choose heaven," the preacher said. "No one would possibly say they'd choose hell. Why don't you come down and accept heaven?"

Goebel couldn't find the courage to stand and walk to the altar. He told his friend he wanted to talk to the preacher. Finally, after a second invitation from the pastor, Goebel walked to the front of the church. The preacher asked him, "Do you know if you're going to heaven?"

"I don't know that I am," Goebel said.

Several people from the congregation knelt around Goebel and prayed with him. One of them told him, "Just ask Jesus to come into your heart."

Goebel prayed, "Lord Jesus, please come into my heart."

Goebel stood after praying and immediately something felt different. He looked at the preacher and said, "Brother Cochran, I know I'm all right."

As Goebel's friend drove him back to his mother's house later that night, he didn't ask him to stop to buy beer at the county line. Once inside his mother's house, Goebel found her sitting alone in a chair in the living room. Since his father had died a few years earlier, Goebel suddenly felt sorry that he had been adding to his mother's sorrow by the way he was living. Goebel knelt before his mother and told her, "Momma, I want you to know that I'm never going to get drunk again. I'm never going to fight again, and I'm never going to get in trouble again."

"Well, what happened?" his mother asked.

"I accepted Jesus Christ into my life tonight," Goebel told her.

The next morning, Goebel woke up early to milk his family's cows. When he finished, he rushed back to the kitchen to share his newly found faith with his mother. Although she didn't accept Jesus Christ as her Savior that morning, she did become a Christian several years later before her death.

As a born-again Christian, Goebel was eager to share with others what he'd experienced in the church the night before. Goebel didn't know much of anything about the Bible, but he knew what God's grace was already doing for him. He didn't want to drink anymore, and he had a new outlook on life. Goebel also knew it was his duty as a Christian to share God's Word with everyone he came in contact with. As Mark 16:15 teaches us, "He said to them, 'Go into all the world and preach the gospel to all creation.'"

Goebel didn't know much of anything about the Bible, but he knew what God's grace was already doing for him.

As Goebel prepared to leave his mother's house the morning after he'd shared his faith with her, he set his sights high. He was going to share the Gospel at Bruno's, which was one of the popular watering holes on U.S. Highway 78. Because Tallapoosa was located between Fort McPherson in Atlanta and Fort McClellan in Anniston, Alabama, Bruno's was a popular pit stop for Army soldiers.

Goebel had spent many mornings at Bruno's, since patrons could buy a mug of beer for a nickel before noon. Now he only had a never-quenching thirst for what was written in the Bible. The bartender, Essie May, was sitting at the corner of the L-shaped bar when Goebel walked in. When Essie May saw him, she reached for a cold mug.

"Essie May, I don't want a beer today," Goebel told her.

"You don't want a beer?" she asked. "Well, what do you want?"

"Essie May, I want to tell you about what happened to me last night," he said.

Goebel started to share his experience with her until she interrupted him. "Wales, I don't want any of that talk in here," she said. "You won't talk like that in here."

"Essie May, I'm a Christian now, and the Lord has forgiven me," he said. "I want you to be a Christian, too."

Two of the three patrons sitting at the bar got up and left. Goebel looked at the remaining man sitting at the bar and noticed tears in his eyes. "You know, what you've been saying to her is what my momma has told me one hundred times," the man said.

"You're not saved?" Goebel asked him.

"No," the man said.

"Well, why didn't you listen to your momma?" Goebel said. "Do you want to be saved now?"

"I think I do," the man said.

"Well, I'm going to tell you what I did in that church last night," Goebel said. "All I did was ask Jesus to come into my heart, and I'm saved this morning. He'll do the same thing for you. Bow your head and ask Him."

The man bowed his head, asked Jesus to come into his heart, and then Essie May ran both of them out of her bar. Years later, Goebel learned that Essie May became a Christian before her death.

Emboldened by his first experience in witnessing to others, Goebel sought to spread the word of God's grace wherever he could. He frequented the many poolrooms, honky-tonks, and beer joints around Tallapoosa to share what he knew to be true with the people who needed it most. He yearned to minister to people who were struggling to overcome the same demons that once consumed his life. But to truly witness to people, Goebel realized he needed to learn as much about the Scripture as he could. His biggest problem: he didn't own a Bible.

Goebel later said, "One of the evidences of being born again is not only to witness to your family and others, but to know the Word of the Lord. You know Him by reading the Word of God. I went to a couple of churches to see if they'd give me a Bible. The Baptist church in town offered to give me one if I agreed to be baptized, but I told them no because it felt like I would have been trading cars or something."

One morning, as Goebel waited outside a honky-tonk for someone to approach, he saw a car pull into a gas station across the highway. As a man climbed out of his car, he told the gas station attendant, "All of this is of the Lord." The man was a Bible salesman from Atlanta.

"You know anyone that might be interested in buying a Bible?" he asked the attendant.

The attendant pointed toward Goebel, who was leaning against a wall across the highway. "You see that tall, lanky guy over there?" the attendant said. "He'll buy a Bible from you."

The man motioned for Goebel to come over. He asked Goebel if he wanted to buy a Bible. When Goebel told him he did, the man asked, "What kind of Bible do you want?"

"I want a big Bible," Goebel said.

Goebel later recalled, "He opened up the trunk, and there were boxes of Bibles in there. I used to carry unholy spirits in the trunk of my car. He carried the Holy Spirit in his."

The man pulled out a brown Bible with a picture of Jesus on the cover. "Who is that?" Goebel asked.

"That's Jesus Christ, son," the man said.

"I was so naive," Goebel later said. "I didn't even know they had pictures of Jesus."

"How much would you sell that Bible for?" Goebel asked.

The man told him the Bible cost twenty-two dollars.

"I don't have that kind of money," Goebel said.

"Well, how much do you have?" the man asked.

"I have two dollars," Goebel said.

"Well, I'll tell you what," the man said. "I'll give you the Bible for two dollars if you promise to send me two dollars every month until it's paid for."

"I'll give you the Bible for two dollars if you promise to send me two dollars every month until it's paid for."

Goebel shook the man's hand and promised to send him the money, which he did. Over the next several months, Goebel became immersed in reading the Scripture and was eager to share what he'd learned. During one visit to a pool hall, Goebel witnessed to a soldier named Harvey who had recently returned home after serving in the Korean War. As Goebel was sharing the Good News with him, Harvey suddenly picked up a pool stick and threatened to hit Goebel with it.

"Harvey, you're not mad at me," Goebel said. "You're mad at my Bible."

Harvey put down the pool stick and left. Afraid Harvey might be outside waiting to attack him, Goebel waited about fifteen minutes before leaving. He found Harvey sitting in his car, weeping. Goebel climbed into the car with him.

"Wales, you're right," Harvey said. "I was offended by your Bible. When I was in Korea, most of the men in my platoon were killed. I promised God that if He got me home, I would live my life for Him. Now, I don't know about everything you're telling me, but I believe if you make a promise, you keep it. What do I need to do?"

"You need to ask Jesus into your heart," Goebel said.

News quickly spread around Tallapoosa about the former bootlegger who was now a budding evangelist. A. L. Jackson, who owned Tallapoosa Mills Lumber Company and lived in one of the stately antebellum homes on Head Avenue, learned about what Goebel was doing. One day, Jackson sent his wife to find him. When she returned home with Goebel, Jackson told him that he believed God had called him to be a preacher, and Jackson offered to pay for Goebel's tuition to seminary if he was willing to go.

"I knew what I wanted to do, and here was a man who was willing to pay for it," Goebel said. "But I couldn't do it. I don't know if I didn't feel worthy or what."

After turning his life around, Goebel returned to West Georgia College and finished his degree. He was also able to win back the girl he had fallen in love with in college. Jean Duff agreed to marry him, and they eventually had three sons. Goebel took a job as a bookkeeper at a Chevrolet dealership and settled down to raise his family. Shortly after Dwight Eisenhower was elected president in 1952, Goebel was offered a job as a U.S. marshal for the Northern District of Georgia. He went to Atlanta for an interview and then waited as the FBI conducted a background check. Although the FBI raised questions about his time as a bootlegger, Goebel was cleared because he'd never been arrested.

While Goebel was excited about the appointment and earning a higher salary, his wife wasn't too thrilled about his new occupation.

"Will you have to carry a gun?" she asked.

"Well, I reckon so," he said.

"Will you have to shoot people?" she asked.

"I don't know," he said.

"Well, I don't like it," she said.

Shortly before Goebel was to start his new job, his brother Seaborn called and offered him a chance for a much safer career. Goebel's brother was a recent graduate of Auburn University with an engineering degree and was about to start building houses in Homewood, Alabama, a bustling suburb of Birmingham. Goebel agreed to take the job and moved his family to Alabama.

Not long after moving to Homewood, the Goebel family started attending Cumberland Presbyterian Church. Soon, Goebel was teaching Sunday school classes and witnessing to people at church and around town. Bill Longshore, a Birmingham attorney, invited Goebel to attend a mission conference in North Carolina, where they listened to the testimony of missionaries from China.

"I would imagine if anything really got me, that was it," Goebel said. "I realized how little I was doing. I began to realize that material things weren't important to me anymore, and God had something more important for me to do. It was an amazing thing."

A short time later, Goebel attended an organizational meeting for Youth for Christ, which was looking to open a chapter in Birmingham. Since Goebel had three sons of his own, he told the group he was interested in being involved. He was quickly elected the group's speaker, even though he hadn't done much public speaking outside of his Sunday school class.

"I didn't think anything of it," Goebel said. "I thought I'd be speaking to small groups of kids. We started having weekly or monthly meetings at churches downtown. Then they started advertising the meetings on the radio, and hundreds of kids started coming."

One of the young girls who attended the meetings regularly was a cheerleader at Ensley High School. She asked Goebel if he would come to the school and speak to her Fellowship of Christian Athletes chapter. FCA had been founded in 1954 by Don McClanen, Eastern Oklahoma A&M basketball coach. Branch Rickey, who is famously known for breaking Major League Baseball's color barrier by signing African American star Jackie Robinson to the Brooklyn Dodgers, helped finance FCA in its first year.

The next week, Goebel spoke to about fifty kids in the music room at Ensley High. One of the boys in attendance was a football player, who told his coach, Herbert Hanes, about Goebel. Coach Hanes invited Goebel to speak to his team one afternoon before practice. At the end of his speech, Goebel invited all the boys to receive Christ when he was finished.

"If you're willing to stand up in front of your buddies, come stand with me," Goebel told them.

A handful of players came to the front of the room. "I felt like Billy Graham," Goebel said. "It was empowering and exciting."

Before long, Goebel was speaking at high schools around the

city. He was one of the most popular speakers at youth revivals organized by Southern Baptists. At W. A. Berry High School, he started a weekly Bible study with the football team, and soon cheerleaders and other students were attending. When Berry High School was planning its religion appreciation week, the principal called Goebel and asked if he'd address the entire student body. "I'm not that kind of speaker," Goebel told him. "I only teach a small Sunday school class."

"Mr. Goebel, this isn't the most popular event of the school year," the principal said. "We have a hard time getting kids to come. You're the first person the students have ever asked for."

"Well, how many kids will be there?" Goebel asked.

"Not too many," the principal said.

When Goebel arrived at Berry High School on the day he was scheduled to speak, the principal told him that they had to move the event out of the gymnasium and to the football stadium because so many kids wanted to attend. When Goebel walked onto the field, there were about three thousand kids sitting in the stands.

As Goebel walked to the podium, he asked the principal, "Have you ever watched Billy Graham? When Billy Graham gets finished, he asks people if they want to come forward and accept Jesus Christ. That's what I'm going to do."

After Goebel finished speaking, about three hundred students accepted his invitation to become Christians. At another rally at Ramsay High School, Goebel spoke to about one thousand students, and more than one hundred kids answered his invitation.

"Wales Goebel was a big, old country boy with a big heart for Jesus," said Hank Erwin, whom Goebel appointed as Woodlawn High's team chaplain. "You have to remember that back in the

1960s, men as big as Wales weren't known for trusting Jesus. To see a guy as big as Wales talking about Jesus was remarkable and fascinating."

In 1967, Goebel left the home construction business and with his wife started the Wales Goebel Ministry, a full-time ministry and counseling service for troubled teenagers. The ministry had nine full-time staff members and operated on donations from churches and individuals. He continued to speak to high school students and expanded his ministry to college campuses. In March 1973, Goebel held a three-day Decision '73 Crusade at the University of Alabama in Tuscaloosa. More than eight hundred student volunteers were involved in planning the crusade, which was held at Memorial Coliseum, the university's basketball arena.

Reigning Miss Alabama Freita Fuller and several NFL players, including Houston Oilers safety Ken Houston, New York Jets center Paul Crane, and Green Bay Packers defensive tackle Mike McCoy, were featured speakers during the crusade. There was a one-thousand-voice choir and other performers. Even legendary Crimson Tide coach Paul "Bear" Bryant endorsed the event in the media. By the time Goebel delivered the closing sermon on the third night, more than ten thousand students had attended the event, including some from as far away as Indiana and Florida.

"About ten years ago I started becoming concerned about our youth," Goebel told *The Tuscaloosa News* during Decision Crusade '73. "I was concerned about drugs and the tendency for youngsters to want to run away from home. So I started sharing a message with young people. I am just so happy that the mood of young people in 1973 has completely changed from the mood of young people in the late 1960s. These young people have seen that sex and drugs are not the answer. They do this because they know Jesus is the answer to their life."

Before the summer was over, Goebel held similar crusades in several cities across the state.

"People came from everywhere to hear him talk about Jesus," Erwin said. "He wasn't shy. What made Wales so adorable was that he didn't know much of the Bible. He would scramble the verses up, but he preached with all of his heart. It got to the point where we said he could read from a phone book and people would come for Christ. He was so passionate about the Lord."

Goebel and Erwin would need all of their passion and more as they prepared for their next challenge. After Goebel spoke to a group of football players at the University of Alabama, one of them approached him to ask for help. He told Goebel that Woodlawn High School desperately needed to hear his message. Woodlawn was the last Birmingham high school to integrate African Americans into its student body, and now a toxic atmosphere surrounded its football team as it prepared for the 1973 season.

A toxic atmosphere surrounded Woodlawn's football team as it prepared for the 1973 season.

As Goebel walked unannounced through Coach Gerelds's office door in August, Gerelds couldn't have known that God would use the tall, bushy-haired son of a German immigrant to save his football team and, more importantly, the lives of many of his players.

CHAPTER FIVE

THE REVIVAL

Shortly after Tandy Gerelds became Woodlawn's head football coach in 1971, government-mandated busing brought more than five hundred African American students to the school. With its *Swann v. Charlotte-Mecklenburg Board of Education* ruling, the U.S. Supreme Court affirmed that federal courts had the jurisdiction to utilize mandatory busing as a means to achieve racial balance in public schools. Gerelds, who had grown up in Birmingham and had never left the state, rarely socialized with African Americans, let alone taught and coached them. In fact, his only previous close interaction with an African American was with his family's maid.

In a testimony he wrote shortly before his death in 2003, Gerelds recalled the challenges of coaching and teaching African Americans for the first time:

> *In 1970, Birmingham city schools were forced to integrate. Five hundred black students were transferred from Hayes High School to Woodlawn. The black students did not want to change schools, and the white students did not want them in their school. This led to bad feelings that soon turned into hatred. I was no different than the students. I had never been around black students, and I did not*

know how to act, coach, or teach them. The only black person that I knew was my maid, Ethel May Porch. Ethel had helped raise me from the time I was three years old. I loved Ethel, but she was the maid and because of her position, she could only be so close to me (my mother made sure she knew her place).

For the next two years, Woodlawn High School became a war zone. Most of the teachers—white and black—quit. Only the strong stayed. The FBI tried to encourage the principal to close the school. He would not. I was attacked, threatened, shot at, and verbally abused constantly. I am saying all of this to explain that my attitudes about teaching and coaching were at an all-time low.

I was made assistant principal because no one else would do it, and the principal asked for help. Not surprising, I became a very hardened person, but I still had an ego to fill as far as coaching. How was I going to get fifty football players, who did not like each other, to play together and win football games? I went about trying. The harder I tried, the worse it seemed to get.

Woodlawn High School, which had been one of the city's football powerhouses during the 1930s, 1940s, and 1950s, was becoming an average football team, as racial tension ripped apart its student body.

Heading into the 1973 season, Gerelds knew it would take a lot of work to turn his program around. He also knew that his job wasn't in danger; who else would want to coach at the racially divided school? In fact, Gerelds might have looked for another job if Woodlawn High had not been his and his wife, Debbie's, alma mater. He loved the school and wasn't ready to surrender, despite so many signs that suggested he should.

In August, Gerelds was willing to try anything to bring his

players together, so he decided the Colonels would have preseason camp at Woodlawn High School. For five days, the Colonels awoke every morning at five, ran one mile before breakfast, practiced three times a day, and then slept on cots in the school's gymnasium. Parents were banned from the school, and players weren't allowed to leave without Gerelds's permission. Gerelds wanted his players to spend every waking moment together. After so much interaction, his players would either learn to get along or become even more divided.

Going into camp, Gerelds didn't know much about his team. He was moving his team's best player, Tony Nathan, from safety to tailback. Nathan wanted no part of running the ball. Besides fullback Mike Allison, safety Bobby Thompson, linebacker Peyton Zarzour, and wingback Roderick Washington, the Colonels didn't have many returning proven players. Most of their starters would be underclassmen who had spent the previous season playing on the B-team and freshman squads. It was Gerelds's job to mold them into a competitive team.

Gerelds was moving his team's best player, Tony Nathan, from safety to tailback. Nathan wanted no part of running the ball.

After the first two days of the preseason camp, Gerelds was disheartened, as his team's chemistry hadn't changed. The white players were sleeping on one end of the gymnasium, while the black players slept on the other side. When the players ate breakfast, lunch, and dinner in the cafeteria, the whites sat together and the blacks sat together. There was very little interaction between races off the practice field. There were nine African American players on the varsity squad: Nathan, fullback Albert Benefield, lineman Reginald Greene, wingback Manuel Jones, linebacker Howard Ross, safety Tommy Rue, lineman Calvin Rumph, defensive end Gary Speers, and wingback Roderick Washington. The other thirty-nine players were white.

"We pushed the kids to the breaking point, and they were showing signs of being very tired and depressed," Gerelds wrote.

In an attempt to build team camaraderie, Gerelds brought in what he hoped would be motivational speakers to address his players after dinner. Former Woodlawn High football star David Langner, who was playing at Auburn University, spoke to the team one night. At the time, Langner was the most beloved (or hated) man in the state.

On December 2, 1972, Langner had famously returned two blocked punts for touchdowns in the fourth quarter of the Tigers' 17–16 victory over rival Alabama in the Iron Bowl at Legion Field in Birmingham. More than four decades later, the game is still known as "Punt Bama Punt." Ironically, Alabama's punter at the time was Greg Gantt, who was Langner's teammate at Woodlawn High. While Woodlawn's players enjoyed Langner's speech, they weren't excited about the Methodist preacher who spoke to them the next night.

On the third day of Woodlawn High's preseason camp, a tall, blond-haired man knocked on Gerelds's door. It was Wales Goebel, youth minister and evangelist from Birmingham, who had heard Gerelds might need his help.

"I want to talk to your players," Goebel said. "I want to talk to them about the Lord."

"I don't think we'll have time," Gerelds said sternly as he

looked back down at the playbook on his desk. "We have our kids in a competitive atmosphere and want to keep it that way."

Goebel, who had encountered his fair share of stubborn and prideful coaches during his work as a youth minister, wasn't about to surrender so easily. Before finding his way to Gerelds's office adjacent to the gym, Goebel had sat in his car in the parking lot outside Woodlawn High. For more than ten minutes, Goebel had prayed—not for the players he wished to address, but that God would open Gerelds's heart so the players could hear what he had to say.

"Let me tell you something: There are two parts of every young person," Goebel said. "There is the physical part and the spiritual part. Based on your results, you're obviously doing a good job with the physical part. But where I come in and where I can help is with the spiritual part. That's why I'm here, and you need to give me thirty minutes with your players."

After staring at Goebel for several seconds, while undoubtedly squinting his eyes to nearly closed as he was apt to do, Gerelds reluctantly agreed to let the stranger talk to his players.

"You can come back after supper," Gerelds said. "You've got thirty minutes."

Goebel wasn't quite ready to leave the young coach.

"Coach, let me ask you something: if you died today, would you go to heaven?" The boldness and, perhaps, the gravity of Goebel's question took Gerelds by surprise. Gerelds's answer betrayed his tough-guy image and revealed an underlying insecurity. Perhaps we're all insecure when we seek to find our identity anywhere other than God. His answer?

"Um, I think I've been pretty good," Gerelds said. "I work hard. Um, I don't know. I don't think anyone can know."

"I know," Goebel said, before walking out of his office.

At dinner, Gerelds informed his players that there would be another speaker addressing them that night. He told his players they were required to be there. After spending the past three days practicing in the sweltering Alabama heat and humidity, listening to another preacher in the non-air-conditioned gym was the last thing the players wanted to do.

"We listened to a Methodist pastor the night before, and he wasn't really inspiring and didn't have a lot to say," said Steve Martin, a junior cornerback. "So when we found out another speaker was coming the next night, everybody was kind of like, 'Oh, great, we've got to do this again.'"

Jerry Stearns, Woodlawn High's defensive coordinator, was worried about what Goebel would say to the team.

"We weren't enthused, to say the least," Stearns said. "I'll be the first to say that some of us said, 'Oh, boy. We've got a Jesus Freak coming tonight.' That's how some of those guys were looked at during that period of time. They weren't the kind of guys that every football coach welcomed into their camp."

With Woodlawn High's players sitting in one section of the wooden bleachers, Goebel's loud, powerful voice soon filled the gym. Goebel talked about his own childhood, how he'd overcome alcoholism as a teenager, and then turned his life around after accepting Jesus Christ as his Lord and Savior. It didn't take him long to get the players' undivided attention.

"Wales can be with you for five minutes and have you eating out of his hand," Stearns said. "He told them funny stories about his childhood, like when he was sipping moonshine in class out of a straw from a bottle in his overalls. All of a sudden, he turns from that and goes into a serious mode. He does it so smoothly and so fast that you don't realize he's changing gears. The next thing you know, he's got you wrapped up in everything he's saying."

"Wales can be with you for five minutes and
have you eating out of his hand."

Goebel shared the story of how he nearly died when he was fifteen years old. While he was riding in a friend's car on Highway 78, a car passing a truck in the opposite lane forced them off the road. Their car hit an embankment and flipped over onto the roof. Goebel and his two friends were trapped, and they saw flames coming from the engine. Goebel remembered crying out to God for help. A convoy of soldiers arrived at the wreck and pulled Goebel and his friends from the car.

"My message was basically a testimony of how Jesus forgives your past sins and gives you a life of peace and direction," Goebel said. "I told them how I was influenced by my father, which most of us are. My father was an atheist and a hard man. As a young boy without any moral compass, I drifted into a lifestyle that would have destroyed my life, as it did with so many of my friends. I was on a fast train going to hell and didn't know how to get off. Churches were plentiful in Tallapoosa, and I'm sure they would have welcomed me. But I didn't know that side of life. The people who went to them were not my kind."

More than anything, Goebel talked to the Woodlawn High players about what God's grace did for him and what it could do for them. Like the preacher who told him about God's plan of salvation in the Methodist church in LaGrange, Georgia, more than two decades earlier, Goebel asked the players if they knew they were going to heaven.

"You've already chosen to be different than the rest of your classmates," Goebel told them. "You've chosen to be a football player at Woodlawn High. You've chosen to make the commitment to be the best you can be, even though there will be broken bones and other injuries involved. Some of you will put in the hard work every day, but may not make the team. Some of you will never see the playing field. I know many of you have goals and aspirations of winning a city championship and going to college. I had those same aspirations. I was good enough to play basketball and phony enough to be elected president of the student body.

"But there comes a time when it all comes to an end and that's eternal. You will come to the end, and you'll find that you won't be satisfied unless you have Jesus Christ in your lives. If you dedicate your life to eternal things—just like you've dedicated yourselves to Coach Gerelds and Woodlawn High School—you have to allow Jesus Christ to come into your heart and life."

Then Goebel asked them the same question he'd considered as a young man: "If you died tonight, do you know where you would go?"

The Woodlawn High gym was silent, and a few of the players shuffled their feet. "As I sat there pondering his words, it was like he was reading my mind," said Reginald Greene, an African American lineman on the team.

"I didn't ask you if you went to church or tried to follow the Ten Commandments the best you can," Goebel told the players. "I asked you if you knew that you would spend eternity in heaven if you died tonight."

"It's exactly what I was thinking," Greene said. "I figured it was what the rest of the team was thinking, too."

"I have good news," Goebel told the players. "If you allow Jesus Christ to come into your heart and life, you will be saved and given eternal life. You have to make a commitment. If you're going to be successful, you have to commit to it now—not later. You've got to commit yourself to Christ. You've got to give yourself to Him before He can really use you. If you're willing to do that and want to do it, then get up and stand with me. We're going to pray to God, and you can let Him into your heart."

Goebel recited Romans 10:9, which teaches, "If you declare with your mouth, 'Jesus is Lord,' and believe in your heart that God raised him from the dead, you will be saved." Then Goebel invited anyone who was ready to receive God's gift of His Son, Jesus Christ, to join Him on the gymnasium floor.

"Wales spoke for about forty-five minutes that night and really presented the case for Christ," said Hank Erwin, who was in the gym that night and would become Woodlawn High's team chaplain. "Then he boldly gave an invitation. It was a really gutsy statement. Nobody knew what was going to happen. The boys were really quiet."

Initially, only a few players climbed down from the bleachers. But then a steady stream of players joined their teammates and Goebel on the floor—white and black players alike. Out of forty-eight players on the team, all but four became Christians that night.

"I remember that one by one they began to get out of their seats and kneel around Wales and make a commitment to Christ," Erwin said. "It was sort of remarkable to see the first few come down, but then it became a trickle, then a stream, and then a wave of all of the athletes coming down. It was remarkable. I think everybody was stunned."

Two players, Steve Martin and defensive end Brad Hendrix, didn't accept Goebel's invitation to become Christians because they'd already been saved. But Martin said Goebel's testimony still had a profound impact on him.

"I think part of it was that he shared his personal testimony," Martin said. "People could respond to and identify with someone who wasn't up there just hanging a blue sky, saying you ought to be a good guy or a nice guy. He talked about the simple life he led up until Christ changed his life. I think that spoke to everybody. It was very powerful to hear what he'd been through and the difference Christ made in his life."

Gerelds, who grew up attending church with his family, didn't have much time for religion and wasn't exactly sure what to make of Goebel. He was more focused on figuring out how to unify his team so it could win football games. As his players gathered around Goebel, Gerelds stood at the top of the bleachers and didn't join them. Although Gerelds would later admit that a strange feeling stirred in his heart and that tears filled his eyes as he listened to Goebel talk about things he'd never heard about God and Jesus Christ, he was too tough to admit he needed help at the time.

"I was not one of them," Gerelds wrote shortly before his death. "I had too much pride to openly admit any weakness. I pretended I was saved and put up a front for the kids."

As Gerelds watched his players and assistant coaches weeping, hugging, and seemingly loving one another, he figured it would soon pass. As he walked down from the top row of the bleachers, he determined that an emotional, religious event would not distract him. He was tough, and he was going to be the best football coach he could possibly be. That meant no distractions and no softness. Still, what he had witnessed seemed real. He felt something inside that he'd never felt before. He planned to go on about his business and figured that the emotional impact of the evening would probably wane as the kids and coaches continued practice and started classes. Gerelds believed that the grind of real life would eventually take its toll.

> Gerelds determined that an emotional,
> religious event would not distract him.

Before leaving the gym, Gerelds shook Goebel's hand and thanked him for coming. "I don't know if this is going to work," Gerelds told him.

"I don't know if it will, either," Goebel said. "But if God's in it, it will work."

That night, Reginald Greene had a difficult time sleeping in the gym. The flying roaches that seemed to be as big as mice were enough to keep him awake, but he lay in his cot for several hours thinking about what he'd done and what it meant. It didn't take very long for Greene and the others to notice a change in their team.

"I saw an athletic change in me the very next day," Greene said. "But even more important, the attitude of the team was completely different. There was a unity and friendship that hadn't existed before—especially between black and white players. That was really something new. Over the next few weeks, there was a transformation in the whole team—mentally, spiritually, and athletically."

Denny Ragland, who was a backup quarterback in 1973, also noticed a significant change in the coaches. There was less screaming and yelling and more teaching and instructing. Even something as trivial as adding ice to the water buckets didn't go unnoticed. The previous year, the Colonels weren't given many water breaks during practice. Now they were getting them every hour.

"I remember being abused by coaches in my earlier years, especially as a freshman and sophomore," Ragland said. "I had been ridiculed verbally, but it all stopped after that night. The relationships became more like they should be, with coaches coaching you and trying to improve you, rather than trying to demean you. Granted, we didn't have the same guys coaching us that we'd had as a freshmen and sophomores, but the fact that they gave us ice in the water blew me away the first time it happened. Practices became not so much about beating people down but about preparing us and setting goals. They treated us more like human beings."

"Practices became not so much about beating people
down but about preparing us and setting goals."

After the meeting in the gym, Goebel instructed his staff member Hank Erwin to return to Woodlawn High as the team's chaplain. "Wales told me he wanted me to go back and teach them what it all means," Erwin said. "I went back and started to figure out how to do it."

Initially, Gerelds and his players weren't very receptive to Erwin's message. They didn't know this man who walked with a limp and stuttered when he was excited. Although Erwin was growing more confident in his faith, he still wasn't as powerful a speaker as Goebel. During the last few days of training camp and in the final weeks of summer break, Erwin talked to Woodlawn's players about what the Lord could do in their lives. He led Bible studies and put a renewed emphasis on the school's Fellowship of Christian Athletes chapter.

Once the players started classes and began serious preparations for the 1973 season, Gerelds was surprised to see that what happened in the gym that night with Goebel was still very much a part of the day-to-day lives of his players and assistant coaches. What Gerelds thought would be a temporary feeling of love and unity hadn't worn off. He noticed that his players did seem to care more about each other. The normal finger-pointing, blame, jealousy, and selfishness that had threatened to rip his team apart was greatly reduced as his team came closer together. The relationships between the black and white players were especially amazing.

Two weeks before the '73 season started, Erwin and the players decided to celebrate the kickoff with an FCA meeting at one of the player's homes. Howie Miller, one of the B-team players, received permission from his parents to host the party at their home in the Crestwood neighborhood of Birmingham. Crestwood was an upper-middle-class section, which meant it was an all-white neighborhood at the time. A few of the players invited Gerelds to attend the party, and he wondered if any of the black players on his team would show up. He wondered if they'd feel uncomfortable or unwelcome at a house in that part of town.

"As I drove into the Crestwood neighborhood, I wondered if any of the black kids had ever been in any of these homes before," Gerelds wrote. "As I walked into the house, I noticed black and white boys with their arms around each other. They were laughing and talking in an honest and sincere way. They were communicating with each other like I always wanted them to do. I felt ignored, as if I was not part of the group. I seemed very unimportant to them. They had the same look on their faces as Wales had when I met him for the first time. After a short stay, I left the party and started home."

At that point in his life, Gerelds had never seen anyone truly give of themselves for the sake of another person. Nor had he done it himself. Suddenly, he was seeing a very real person (Christ) living *His* life out in the lives of sixteen-, seventeen-, and eighteen-year-olds. Though his players were from a variety of backgrounds—some rich, some poor, some black, some white—they had learned that their differences didn't matter. They loved each other.

What Gerelds witnessed at that FCA gathering was something he'd never seen before. He saw white players and black players standing arm in arm. The players and their parents were truly enjoying one another. No one had an agenda. They were there for one another, encouraging, praying, singing, and loving each other. For a young, ambitious coach, it was peculiar—but it was even oddly inviting.

Gerelds knew that what he'd seen was real, and he knew he didn't have what those young men on his team had. The reality was that he didn't have Who they now had in their lives. As Gerelds drove home that night, he started speaking up to the sky. He confessed to God that he wasn't sure about many things in the world, but he was sure of the difference he'd seen in the lives of the young men he'd been with over the past several weeks. Gerelds pulled his car into his driveway, went into the house, and headed straight to his bedroom. He knelt next to his bed and spoke to the God of the universe. For the first time in his life, he was certain there was a Father there who loved him. Gerelds met Jesus that night and was never the same. While he would wait until after the 1973 season to be baptized at Huffman Assembly of God Church, he knew love now, and now he knew how to love.

"The Lord did in five seconds what I had tried to do sixteen hours a day for two years. He made a football team out of individuals."

"As I drove home, I began to think about what Wales had said that night," Gerelds wrote. He went on to say:

He spoke of being humble and coming to the Lord as a child. When I got home, I got down on my knees and asked the Lord to give me what He gave those kids. I told Him that I didn't care about winning football games and impressing others. All I wanted was to feel like the players felt. The Lord came into my life that night and gave me what He gave the players: love. The Lord did in five seconds what I had tried to do sixteen hours a day for two years: he made a football team out of individuals.

And the Woodlawn High School Colonels were about to find out that they'd never be the same.

CHAPTER SIX

THE CHAPLAIN

During Hank Erwin's sophomore year at Troy State University in Troy, Alabama, in 1969, he fell to his knees on the floor of his dormitory room. A once promising college baseball player, Erwin wasn't sure he could play the game he loved any longer because of the excruciating and never-ending pain in his right foot. A few months earlier, as Erwin worked a summer job at a steel mill in Fairfield, Alabama, a steel beam crushed his right foot.

Initially, doctors wanted to amputate Erwin's right leg up to the knee. But he persuaded the doctors to only amputate half of his right foot; he told them they could come back later and take the rest if necessary. Erwin was hospitalized for the next two months, and doctors were encouraged as his body fought off infection. When Erwin was discharged from the hospital, doctors told him he would walk with a severe limp, couldn't run, and, of course, would never play baseball again.

"My life was all about baseball, and it went up in a puff of smoke," Erwin said. "I found myself asking the big questions of life, like *What do you do when your dream goes up in flames?*"

At least Hank Erwin didn't have to go far to find encouragement and inspiration. His father, Henry Eugene "Red" Erwin Sr., was a World War II hero who had been awarded the Medal of

Honor for his heroism that saved the crew of his B-29 Superfortress as it flew a bombing mission over Japan on April 12, 1945. Red Erwin, who was a radio operator on the B-29 called *City of Los Angeles*, was also responsible for dropping phosphorus smoke bombs through a chute on the floor of the plane when it reached enemy territory.

On the morning of Red's eleventh combat mission, the B-29 was supposed to bomb a chemical plant at Koriyama, about 120 miles north of Tokyo. As the plane was being bombarded by antiaircraft fire, Red was given the signal to start dropping the smoke bombs. He pulled a pin and dropped a bomb into the chute. The bomb's fuse malfunctioned and ignited the phosphorus, which was burning at 1,100 degrees. The canister flew back up the chute and into Red's face, blinding him, searing off one of his ears, and badly burning his nose.

As Red cradled the bomb between his bare
right arm and ribs, the phosphorus burned
through his flesh and set his body on fire.

Smoke quickly filled the B-29's cockpit, and Red feared the bomb would burn a hole through the floor of the bomb bay. Unable to see, he picked up the bomb and crawled toward the co-pilot's window. As Red cradled the bomb between his bare right arm and ribs, the phosphorus burned through his flesh and set his body on fire. Somehow, he stumbled into the cockpit, tossed the bomb out the window, and then collapsed between the pilots' seats.

The B-29 crew flew Red to Iwo Jima for medical treatment. The doctors there were convinced he wouldn't survive the night. After learning of Red's heroism, Army Air Force officials approved awarding him the Medal of Honor while he was still alive. A medal was flown from Guam to Iwo Jima for the bedside ceremony.

Miraculously, Red survived his injuries. He was flown back to the United States and underwent forty-one surgeries over the next thirty months. Doctors were able to restore his eyesight, and he regained use of his left arm. For thirty-seven years, Red worked as a benefits counselor at the Veterans Hospital in Birmingham. He was an inspiration to injured veterans until his death on January 16, 2002.

"His character was the biggest thing," Hank Erwin said. "Dad was a very humble man. He never lied, cheated, or stole a thing. He hated debt. He never cursed and he never drank. He loved America. He wanted to honor the Medal of Honor. He believed in excellence in everything."

So, as Erwin knelt on the floor of his dormitory room at Troy State University—contemplating the probable loss of his promising baseball career—he recalled the lessons of perseverance and determination he'd learned from his father. Erwin hadn't totally given up on his baseball career after his injury; he'd fought hard enough to run and pitch again. But the pain in his right foot was so unbearable that he was beginning to think it was too much to overcome. Then he remembered the seemingly insurmountable odds his father faced.

"My father never griped about it and never said, 'Why me?'" Erwin said. "He always said, 'I survived the war. I knew a lot of guys who didn't come back.' He was thankful. He was a towering figure of influence and a measurement of what men could be like."

For the first time in his life, Erwin prayed to God for strength and direction.

"God, I don't even know if You're real," Erwin prayed. "I don't know if Jesus is real, but if You can make me happy and change my life, You can have it. Whatever I have to do, come into my life, be my personal Savior, be the Lord of my life, and whatever You want, I'll do."

That night, Erwin slept better than he had in a long time.

"It's all I knew to do," Erwin said. "I didn't know much about the Bible and didn't know much background. But the Lord honored my prayer. I didn't see any chairs rumbling across the floor and didn't hear angels. But I felt a peace that I'd never felt before. Over the next few weeks and months, the Lord did little things to let me know that He'd heard my prayer and had accepted it on face value."

Despite the pain in his leg, Erwin was able to finish his baseball career at Troy State. As his right leg became stronger, his velocity returned, and he became a much more effective pitcher. Something else about Erwin changed dramatically, too. Before Erwin's prayer, he was an introverted young man—deeply shy, perhaps because he had a severe stuttering problem that began in childhood. But as Erwin grew stronger in his faith, he became a more confident speaker, and his stuttering mostly stopped.

"When Jesus changed my life, He also changed my heart and my outlook," Erwin said. "And He changed my speech. It was like the shell broke off. I started enjoying people and enjoying life. People would say: 'Here comes happy Hank Erwin.'"

Erwin used baseball—he was able to continue playing by fighting through the pain in his foot—as an opportunity to share with others how God was changing his life. He started attending Fellowship of Christian Athletes meetings and then joined Campus Crusade for Christ, which was founded by Bill Bright in 1951 as a ministry for college students at the University of California, Los Angeles.

"I wondered if there were other players on my team who were like me," Erwin said. "I started going down the roster one by one and sharing Christ with them. Some rejected it and thought I was off my rocker, but some accepted Christ. As a result, our bond and performance level went up like never before. I began to wonder what would happen if an entire team accepted Christ. I always kept that in the back of my mind."

"I began to wonder what would happen if an entire team accepted Christ."

Erwin expanded his on-campus ministry and helped organize Challenge Life, a church-oriented organization, which met on campus every Sunday night. It grew from only three students at the first meeting to more than three hundred in just a few months. At one meeting, Erwin noticed a pretty blond girl, Shelia Daniel, who was leading the ladies' Bible study. She had a boyfriend at the time, but Erwin started dating her after the couple broke up. They went on several dates in December 1971 and were married the next year.

"I'd been praying to the Lord, asking to find a girl who had a special love for Jesus that was beyond the normal love," Erwin said.

Together, Erwin and his young wife helped spread the message of Jesus Christ and God's saving grace on the Troy State campus. Erwin met Wales Goebel, a popular youth minister from Birmingham, who made a lasting impression on him. At the time, America was still heavily involved in the Vietnam War—Saigon wouldn't fall until April 30, 1975—and the antiestablishment and hippie counterculture of sex, drugs, and rock 'n' roll was flourishing among the country's youth.

It had been nearly a decade since President John F. Kennedy was shot and killed in Dallas on November 22, 1963, and four years since his brother Robert Kennedy and civil rights leader Martin Luther King Jr. were assassinated within three months of each other in 1968. Six days after King was murdered by a white supremacist in Memphis, Tennessee, African Americans rioted in Washington, D.C., Baltimore, Chicago, and dozens of other U.S. cities. The civil rights struggle was an international black eye for the United States, and anxiety over atomic weapons still weighed heavily on the minds of most Americans. The country's political unrest reached its pinnacle at the 1968 Democratic convention in Chicago, where antiwar protesters clashed with police.

Time magazine later called 1968 "a knife blade that severed past from future . . . the more complicated Now that began when the U.S. saw that it was losing a war it should not have been fighting in the first place, when the huge tribe of the young revolted against the nation's elders and authority, and when the nation finished killing its heroes."

"The '60s were what I would call a cauldron of change," Erwin said. "If there was any era that was the basic pivot point of the United States and its culture, it was the 1960s. We had just come out of World War II and most of our daddies were veterans. There was a lot of patriotism and flag-waving going into the 1960s. But when we got into the Vietnam War, there was a shift in patriotism. It was a war no one wanted. It kept escalating. You had an era of international focus on Vietnam, and America being drawn into it. It was a time when your dreams were being battered by the realization that you might have to go to war. We were tired of war. It all came to a head on the streets. It was the left versus the right, and old America versus new America. We all wondered if America would survive."

During this time of turmoil, something called the Jesus People Movement began spreading like wildfire on college campuses from coast to coast. Led by the "Jesus People" and the "Jesus Freaks," Christianity was suddenly becoming a popular alternative to the antiwar movement of the '60s. Instead of smoking marijuana and dropping LSD, many flower children were getting high on Jesus. While it's unclear exactly who started the Jesus People Movement, many historical accounts credit the 1968 opening of a small storefront evangelical mission called the Living Room, in San Francisco's Haight-Ashbury district. A young Bay area couple, Ted and Liz Wise, and other Christian families opened the Living Room to minister to the street people of the district.

Instead of smoking marijuana and dropping LSD, many flower children were getting high on Jesus.

The Living Room opened in the same area of San Francisco that spawned the hippie counterculture and 1967's Summer of Love. Members of psychedelic rock groups like the Grateful Dead and Jefferson Airplane lived within a short distance of the intersection of Haight and Ashbury Streets.

Soon thereafter, other missions, Christian coffeehouses, and commune houses opened on the West Coast. Arthur Blessitt, who is perhaps best known for carrying a cross through every country of the world, opened a coffeehouse called His Place next door to a topless go-go club in Hollywood. He ministered to hippies, Hell's Angels, and would-be actors and became known as the "Minister of Sunset Strip." Around the same time, Chuck Smith, pastor of Calvary Chapel in Costa Mesa, allowed a long-haired convert named Lonnie Frisbee to move into his house. Frisbee brought so many converts home that thirty-five men were soon living in their house, and many of them were baptized in the Pacific. Smith and Frisbee called their commune the House of Miracles, and they eventually opened 187 of their Shiloh communities around the country.

Kent Philpott, a student at Golden Gate Baptist Theological Seminary, opened the Soul Inn in Haight-Ashbury, along with David Hoyt, a former Hare Krishna. Jack Sparks, a former Campus Crusade for Christ missionary at the University of California, Berkeley, formed the Christian World Liberation Front and published one of the first Jesus People newspapers, *Right On!*. In Seattle, Linda Meissner, a young Methodist evangelist from rural Iowa, organized the Jesus People Army. Her group soon grew to include more than five thousand members, and she opened a counseling center called the Ark, and then the Catacombs, a Jesus People coffeehouse, near the Space Needle.

"Kids still walked around in blue jeans and tie-dyed shirts," Erwin said. "But instead of trying to burn things down, they were embracing Jesus. The national media called them 'Jesus Freaks.' Instead of doing drugs, they were doing Jesus."

About a year before Erwin was married, he and his future wife registered for Explo '72, short for Spiritual Explosion, which was a six-day evangelistic conference in Dallas sponsored by Campus Crusade for Christ. Ten days after they were married, Hank and Shelia Erwin left for their honeymoon at Explo '72. Once they arrived in Dallas with a group of students from Troy State, the newly married couple attempted to check into their hotel. They'd called the conference organizers in advance to tell them they were now married and wanted to room together. For whatever reason, the hotel didn't have a reservation for them.

"The hotel was packed," Erwin said. "There wasn't a room left. In fact, there wasn't a hotel room left in Dallas. The lady at the front desk told us we'd have to stay with others. I looked at my new wife and she had tears in her eyes. This was our honeymoon."

As the Erwins started to walk away in disappointment, the telephone at the front desk rang. The clerk answered and then signaled for them to wait.

"I've got good news," she told them. "We have a room—if the newlywed suite will be sufficient."

"We'll take it!" Shelia Erwin screamed.

On the first night of their honeymoon, about eighty thousand other college students from all over the United States and seventy-five other countries surrounded Hank and Shelia Erwin as they sat in the Cotton Bowl. The students, who flocked to Dallas as if on a pilgrimage, were mostly white, largely middle-class, and heavily conservative.

"It was my first time in the Cotton Bowl, and I'll never forget looking at the whole stadium and seeing that it was completely full," Erwin said. "The whole field was covered, and it was a sea of people. I'll never forget the sight of so many young people coming together from across the country. It was etched in my mind that this was an unbelievable moment in history."

With a presidential election looming that fall, President Richard Nixon asked to speak at the event, but Bill Bright—founder of Campus Crusade for Christ and one of the sponsors of this event—turned down his request. He did, though, read a telegram from Nixon on the event's opening night, in which the president told those in attendance, "The way to change the world for the better is to change ourselves for the better through . . . deep and abiding commitment to spiritual values." On the last day of Explo '72, five men were caught breaking into the Democratic Party headquarters at the Watergate complex in Washington, D.C.

Over the next five days, the Erwins attended evangelism and discipleship training, Bible study classes, and other seminars during the morning. They went door-to-door in Dallas spreading the Gospel in the afternoon and then were back at the Cotton Bowl each night to hear musical acts, well-known preachers, professional athletes, and other Christian celebrities. The Reverend Billy Graham addressed the crowd six times.

On the last day of the conference, a crowd estimated to be between one hundred and two hundred thousand people gathered on a huge tract of rain-soaked mud north of downtown Dallas for a "Jesus Music Festival." It was dubbed the "Christian Woodstock" by the press. The performers included Johnny Cash, Kris Kristofferson, Larry Norman, and Children of the Day. As students sang and danced to the bands, many of them pointed their index fingers to the sky, mimicking the popular "one way" symbol of the Jesus Movement.

Explo '72 made a lasting impression on Erwin—one he would carry with him to Woodlawn High School in Birmingham, Alabama.

"The message of Explo '72 was quite simple: people need Christ," Erwin said. "If you want to change the world, help bring people to Christ. The more people you bring to Christ, the more you can change the world. It resonated because young people wanted to do something, wanted to make a difference, and wanted to make their lives count. They wanted to do it in a way that was positive. We wanted it to have a lasting effect."

After returning to Birmingham to start his life with his new bride, Erwin was hired as youth director at Shades Mountain Independent Church. He attended classes at Southeastern Bible College to learn more about Scripture. Erwin started working closely with Goebel at youth Bible studies and eventually agreed to accept a full-time position at Wales Goebel Ministry. Erwin helped organize a Challenge '72 revival at his alma mater, with students packing the school's gymnasium to hear Goebel preach.

Then on a hot, humid August day in 1973, Goebel called Erwin and asked him to meet him at the gymnasium at Woodlawn High School. Goebel was going to speak to Woodlawn's football team and needed Erwin's help.

"I had a tremendous amount of enthusiasm going into that meeting," Erwin said. "I knew we were going to change the world for Christ. I was so excited about the potential and the future. I knew great adventures were coming. Once we walked into the gymnasium at Woodlawn High School, history began to change."

CHAPTER SEVEN

"CHICKEN BIG"

Steve Martin, a defensive back at Woodlawn High during the early '70s, remembers the first time he saw Tony Nathan on the football field. Martin and Nathan were teammates on the Colonels' freshman team in 1971.

"He was the best athlete I'd ever been around," Martin said. "He could play anything. He was incredible. In a lot of ways, it was like a man playing with boys. He was bigger, faster, and stronger and was an incredible athlete. He was probably 190 pounds and could run like a deer."

The only problem: Nathan didn't want any part of running with the football. And, more important, his mother didn't want him even touching the football.

When Nathan informed his mother, Louise, that he wanted to try out for Woodlawn's football team, she told Coach Tandy Gerelds to make sure her son was as far away from the football as possible.

"I never liked football until Tony started playing," Louise Nathan said. "I didn't have a problem with baseball or basketball, but all I ever saw in football was everybody piling on top of somebody. I never wanted him to play on a team."

Despite having never played organized football, Nathan made

the B-team as a freshman and started at safety on defense. He didn't play on offense and stood on the sideline when the Colonels had the ball, even though he was easily the team's most gifted runner. Nathan was equally talented as a defensive back and always seemed to be in position to intercept passes. But instead of catching the ball, Nathan knocked it down so he wouldn't have to run with it. When he mustered the courage to intercept a pass—and disobey his mother's wishes—he ran straight toward the sideline to avoid would-be tacklers.

Tony Nathan was easily the team's most gifted runner.

Above all else, his mother wanted him to avoid being tackled—and Tony wasn't about to disobey his momma.

"My mom didn't want me to play football in the beginning," Nathan said. "Eventually, I and everyone else brought her to where she was comfortable with it. She told my coach to put me as far away from the ball as possible."

From the start, Coach Gerelds recognized that Nathan could be a very special player. For Nathan to reach his full potential, though, Gerelds knew he had to win the trust of his parents. Winning over William "Pops" Nathan II would be easy because the man had never met a stranger. But Louise Nathan was a big, vocal, strong-willed woman who believed her son was better suited to play less violent sports.

Tony's father grew up near Dayton in Marengo County, Alabama. Tony's grandfather was a farmer, and Pops and his six brothers and one sister grew up picking cotton on the family's farm. Tony's father, called "Pops" by his children, loved sports from an early age. His all-black high school didn't have a gymnasium, so he played basketball on a sand court and baseball in the cotton fields. As an annual Fourth of July holiday tradition, Pops and his brothers challenged a team of neighborhood kids in a baseball game. Pops's father taught his sons to place cotton in front of the bases and home plate; the soft, fluffy white clouds helped them slide into the bases more easily.

After graduating from high school, Pops served two years in the Army. He left the military in 1955 and was headed to Chicago, where he accepted a job as a welder. But while visiting one of his brothers in Birmingham, Pops figured out he didn't want to live in a place that was so cold during the winter, so he decided to stay in Birmingham and took a job forming and pouring concrete.

Shortly before moving to Birmingham, Pops met Louise Williams, whose sister was dating one of his brothers. Louise was only fifteen years old, but Pops won over her parents, who agreed to let the couple marry. They were married on Christmas Day 1955. Nearly sixty years later, Pops likes to joke that he chose Christmas Day as their wedding date so it would be easier for him to remember his anniversary. He paid five dollars for a marriage license and gave the preacher four dollars for conducting the ceremony. Pops took his young wife to Birmingham, where they moved into a small, sparsely furnished one-bedroom apartment with a refrigerator, two-eye stovetop, and a bed. After seeing the apartment for the first time, Louise asked her husband, "You brought me to this?"

"Yes," Pops told her. "But it will get better as we grow."

Before too long, their expanding family would need a bigger place. A son, Tony Curtis Nathan, was born on December 14, 1956. Their daughter, Diane, was born two years later, and then came two more boys, Vince and Cedric. When Tony was about eleven years old, his parents adopted Louise's younger sister, Erma Gean. Erma Gean was only two years older than Tony, and although she was his aunt, it didn't take her long to fit right in with the other kids.

The Nathan family moved into a bigger home in Zion City near the city's airport and then to the Center Point neighborhood. By then, Pops was working the graveyard shift at Conner Steel, one of the biggest plants in Birmingham's booming steel industry. Louise was a homemaker and cared for the couple's five children. She taught herself how to sew and became a seamstress to make extra money by sewing for others. She also saved money by making her children's clothes. Tony liked to joke that his clothes were originals and no one else could buy them. His mother even made him a mint green tuxedo for his senior prom and a matching dress for his date.

"She was the boss," Tony said. "She was spunky. She was a big-boned woman with a big frame and didn't play. She was a disciplinarian and got her point across."

The Nathan children were required to complete daily chores, and there were consequences if they didn't. Tony and his siblings were expected to attend church and Sunday school every week. If they were too sick or too tired to go to church, they couldn't do anything else that day. Tony spent most of his childhood days playing basketball, baseball, and football with other kids from his neighborhood. They swam in nearby Village Creek, which was only about waist-deep and separated his neighborhood from an all-white subdivision. Tony rarely went to the creek alone.

"If you were caught in the creek, you were stoned," Tony said. "If the white cats caught us in the water, they would run us out of there. If we caught the white cats in there, we ran them out. It wasn't that we hated anybody, that's just the way it was. That was the norm and that's what you did."

"If the white cats caught us in the water, they would run us out of there. If we caught them there, we ran them out."

When school was out, Tony and his siblings spent most of their summer break working on their grandfather's farm near Union Town, Alabama. There, under the scorching sun, they were taught the valuable lesson that nothing comes easy. For eight hours a day, Tony and his brothers and sisters picked cotton, hoed weeds, and tended to animals. His grandfather William Nathan awoke every morning at four. By the time his grandchildren were up, he had already completed his chores. Tony picked cotton and worked in the field until noon, and then his aunt brought them lunch. Then they'd go back to filling sacks of cotton until sunset.

"I didn't know what I wanted to do with my life at the time," Tony said. "But I knew what I didn't want to do. I didn't want to pick cotton anymore. It was hard work and really made me respect my grandfather."

It was on his mother's father's farm that Tony learned how to run. Erma Gean, who was still living with his maternal grandparents, chased Tony through the fruit trees and across the cotton fields. By the time Erma Gean was done with Tony, his legs were usually tired and aching.

For the most part, Tony's parents sheltered him and his siblings from the racial violence in Birmingham during the 1960s and early 1970s. Even though civil rights protests, marches, and bombings were happening all around them, the violence was rarely discussed in their home. In fact, the only time it was mentioned was after one of the children saw the violence on the TV news. After watching TV one day, Tony asked his father, "Why does this stuff happen?"

"If I knew why, I would fix it," Pops told him. "But who knows how long it would take to fix? People don't like other people because they look different. Some people just have hatred in their hearts."

Pops and Louise tried to teach their children the Golden Rule, which was taught by Jesus in Luke 6:31: "Do to others as you would have them do to you." Both of Tony's parents had a deep conviction of the truth and reality of the Gospel as taught in the New Testament of the Bible. They knew God loved them through Jesus Christ. Therefore, they didn't need everyone else to love them. Louise attended a few civil rights meetings, where she listened to Dr. Martin Luther King share his biblical stance of nonviolent protest and turning the other cheek to the injustice that African Americans faced in the South. She tried to teach her children to live above the hatred as well. Even though there were plenty of times Tony and his brothers and sisters may have wanted to shout, scream, or punch people for the way they were treated, they were taught to find a peaceful solution.

"My father taught me to walk away," Tony said. "He told me not to turn my back to them, but to walk away. He told me not to start anything, but if I had to finish it, to finish it. My mom was big on that one—don't ever start a fight, but if you have to finish it, you better finish it."

It was a valuable lesson for Tony as he prepared to enroll at Woodlawn High in September 1971. By then, Woodlawn was desegregated and African American students were being bused in from Tony's neighborhood. His aunt Erma Gean, who was a junior when Tony started his freshman year, was among the first black students to attend Woodlawn. She wanted to attend all-black Hayes High School but was required to transfer to Woodlawn during forced integration. She wasn't happy about attending a new school, especially one where she wasn't welcome.

Erma Gean was tough, but her experience at Woodlawn High was far more volatile than what her younger nieces and nephews would face at their new school. Like Tony's mother, Erma Gean was strong-willed and big-boned. Most people who crossed paths with Erma Gean were afraid of her, as she was a little slower to adopt Dr. King's principles of restraint. But her reputation helped pave the way for the younger ones who followed her. When Tony enrolled at Woodlawn High as a freshman, most of the students left him alone because they knew he was Erma Gean's nephew. It didn't hurt that he also was one of the best athletes in the school.

Most people were afraid of Erma Gean, as she was a little slower to adopt Dr. King's principles of restraint.

"Nobody in the neighborhood messed with Gean, and because of Gean, nobody messed with me," Tony said. "She was a great person, but she wasn't going to take much from anybody.

She'd let it go for a while, but then she'd get physical. During the first few weeks after busing began, my mother had to go to the school quite a few times because of problems with Gean."

After growing up in an all-black neighborhood and attending a segregated grammar school, Tony came face-to-face with racism for the first time at Woodlawn High. Even though Woodlawn was integrated, seating in the classes was still segregated. The white students sat on one side of the classroom and the blacks on the other, with an empty row between them. As racial tension continued to increase at the beginning of the 1971–72 school year, police officers with dogs patrolled the hallways. For a while, white students were released first to go to their next classes, while black students waited for them to clear the hallways.

"People would look at you like they were amazed you were there," Tony said. "It was like learning on the job. You'd meet people and they'd show you how you needed to deal with them. You could look at them, read their demeanor, and hear what they say. Then you'd know how to deal with them."

Sports became his refuge from the racial problems that plagued Woodlawn High. Shortly before school started, Tony reluctantly tried out for the football team because a few friends from his neighborhood decided to play. Tony had never played football on an organized team. His only exposure to the sport had been in backyard games with other kids from the neighborhood. The boys played in the Nathans' yard so much that his father eventually gave up trying to grow a lawn. When Tony asked his mother if he could join Woodlawn's freshman team, she reluctantly gave him permission to play with one caveat—he had to be as far away from the football as possible.

It didn't take Tony's teammates and coaches long to figure out that he might become a pretty special football player. Denny Ragland, a freshman quarterback at Woodlawn in 1971, remembers a group of black basketball players showing up to watch the football B-team practice one day. "Why are you out here?" Ragland asked one of them. "Why do you care about B-team football?"

The boy pointed at Tony, who was playing free safety, which was literally as far away from the football—and the action—as he could possibly be.

"He's not going to play football," the boy said. "He's already an All-American basketball player."

Indeed, Tony's first love was basketball. His father was a big baseball fan and tried to steer his son toward that sport. Pops was a big fan of the Atlanta Braves and especially outfielder Hank Aaron. Pops took his sons to Atlanta at least once every summer to watch the Braves play. Tony played baseball at Woodlawn High—Colonels defensive coordinator Jerry Stearns recalled him being the only player to ever hit a home run over the old scoreboard at Rickwood Field—but it was never his favorite sport.

"Basketball was more exciting to me," Tony said. "There was a lot more movement by a lot more people. It also didn't help that I hadn't learned how to hit a curveball."

Tony was a naturally gifted athlete, and it didn't take him long to become a star on Woodlawn High's football team. He was the best player on the B-team and was ready to move up to the varsity squad as a sophomore. However, when preseason camp started in August 1972, Tony noticed that most of his African American friends weren't out there with him. They'd either quit or been cut from the team. Tony imagined them being back in his neighborhood, playing basketball or swimming in Village Creek without him. So Tony jogged off the practice field and went home. When he walked through the front door of his house, his mother was waiting for him.

"Why aren't you at football practice?" she asked.

"I quit the team," he said.

"You did what?" she asked.

"Well, I quit playing football," he said.

"Today? Why?" she asked.

"Well, uh . . ."

"Oh, no," she said. "That ain't happening. I've never known a Nathan to quit, and you're not going to be the first. Go get in the car."

"Where are we going?" Tony asked her.

"You're going back to the school," she said.

Louise Nathan found Gerelds and the other coaches in their offices. She instructed Tony to apologize to Gerelds for missing practice. Then Tony asked his coach if he would allow him back on the team.

"You do what you need to do with him as far as punishment," Louise said. "He's yours—but keep him as far away from the football as possible."

During the next few weeks of preseason practice, Gerelds and Stearns decided Tony was their best option to play free safety on the varsity team. Because Tony refused to run with the ball or even play on offense, Jimmy Williams, another assistant coach, gave him a not-so-coveted nickname. Williams had already nick-named another player "Chicken Little" because he was so afraid of getting hit. Tony was much bigger and stronger, but he didn't like contact, either.

"Tony, you've got to stay on the field, son," Williams told him. "You can't run for the sideline every time you touch the ball. We've already got a 'Chicken Little.' I guess you're going to be 'Chicken Big.'"

"Tony, you've got to stay on the field, son. You can't run for the sideline every time you touch the ball."

The Colonels opened the '72 season against Robert E. Lee High School at the Cramton Bowl in Montgomery, Alabama. The Cramton Bowl was one of the state's most historic stadiums. With a seating capacity of 24,000, the Cramton Bowl had hosted University of Alabama games in the past, as well as the annual Blue-Gray Football Classic, a college all-star game. On September 23, 1927, the Cramton Bowl was the site of the very first football game played under the lights in the South.

Robert E. Lee High was one of the state's powerhouses in football. The Generals won back-to-back Class 4A state championships in 1969 and 1970. They went 12–0 in 1969, including a 28–13 victory over Woodlawn High in the first round of the state playoffs, and then 13–0 in 1970. The Generals won 27 games in a row until tying Jeff Davis High School in a 14–14 stalemate on September 17, 1971. The Generals produced many future college stars, including tailbacks Ralph Stokes (Alabama) and Paul Spivey (Alabama), guard John Rogers (Alabama), tackle Herb Broom (Auburn), and defensive end Lee Gross (Auburn). The Generals slipped to a 7–2–1 record in 1971, but they were still bringing back a team that was much bigger, faster, and stronger than the Colonels.

When Gerelds led his team out of the locker room at the Cramton Bowl on September 1, 1972, he noticed that the Generals were already on the field for pregame warm-ups. Gerelds didn't want his players to notice how much bigger the Generals were, so he marched his team around the stands to the other side of the field. That way, the Colonels wouldn't see what was about to hit them.

Shortly after the game started, the Generals took a 3–0 lead on a 37-yard field goal. The Colonels answered on their next possession, tying the score at 3–3 on Raymond "Buzzy" Walsh's 22-yard field goal. It was the only scoring until midway through the fourth quarter. With Nathan playing free safety, Woodlawn's defense shut down Robert E. Lee's vaunted running game. The Generals had averaged more than 300 rushing yards per game the previous season, but the Colonels held them to only 96 rushing yards in the game. Woodlawn's defense also intercepted three passes and picked up two fumbles.

With about seven minutes left in the fourth quarter, Lee attempted to run an option play to the right. The Colonels forced a fumble, and Nathan came out of nowhere to scoop up the ball and return it 38 yards for a touchdown. Walsh's point-after kick gave Woodlawn a 10–3 lead. The Colonels intercepted two passes in the final minutes to secure an unlikely 10–3 victory.

Sometime around ten o'clock that night, the telephone started ringing off the hook at the Nathan home. Louise didn't attend the game because the brakes on her car weren't working properly. Pops skipped the game to go coon hunting, which was how he spent most of his weekends during the fall. After learning from friends what her son had done that night, Louise vowed never to miss another one of Tony's games and she never did.

On Labor Day 1972, *The Birmingham News* ran the headline "Jury Still Out on How Good Colonels Are." After upsetting the mighty Generals in the opener, Gerelds knew his team was going to be better than maybe even he believed. But he wasn't sure it was quite ready to compete for a city championship.

"I don't know," Gerelds told the newspaper. "We'll have to wait and see. I'll say this: I believe our defense is for real. I knew when the season started we were capable of being a better ball club. Most of our good players are back from last year. We're bigger, and stronger, and quicker."

The next week, Woodlawn High played undefeated Hayes High School at Lawson Field in Birmingham. The Colonels jumped on the Pacesetters early, scoring 22 points in the first quarter. Quarterback Jimmy Hammock scored on a 63-yard run and then threw a 60-yard touchdown to tailback Curtis Dixon. Fullback Lloyd Alford closed the scoring with a two-yard plunge. Woodlawn High's offense didn't do much the rest of the game, but its defense shut down Hayes High for a 22–6 victory.

After a 2–0 start, the Colonels were No. 11 in Class 4A in the state rankings. The next week, Woodlawn shut out Vestavia Hills 14–0 in a game that was closer than expected. The Colonels stumbled on offense, throwing two interceptions and losing two fumbles, but their defense held the Rebels to 151 yards and forced four turnovers.

Gerelds was more than satisfied with his defense after three games, especially end Kirk Price and linebacker Bubba Holland. Woodlawn had allowed a total of nine points in three games and was one of only four unbeaten teams left in Birmingham. If the Colonels didn't get better on offense, though, Gerelds knew his team wouldn't stay undefeated for long.

"Our defensive unit has held us together through the last couple of games, while our offense has been sputtering," Gerelds told *The Birmingham News*. "We've got to start doing a lot of things better than we've been doing them."

In a 20–6 victory over Ramsay High School on September 29, Nathan intercepted three passes and made two open-field tackles that might have prevented the other team from scoring two touchdowns. He was quickly becoming one of the best defensive backs in the state. The Colonels took an early 20–0 lead over the Rams, but then once again sputtered on offense in the second half.

On the first Friday night of October, the Colonels faced their toughest challenge so far against undefeated Huffman High School, which was ranked No. 7 in the state. The Colonels had climbed to No. 6 in the state rankings, but Gerelds wasn't sure his team was good enough on offense to challenge the Vikings.

The Colonels faced their toughest challenge so far against undefeated Huffman High School, which was ranked No. 7 in the state.

"Last year Huffman had some good players and some more with a lot of potential," Gerelds told the *News* a few days before the game. "This year those great players are back, and the others have realized their potential with a year of experience. In short, they have outstanding athletes at every position. We take a lot of pride in our defense here at Woodlawn, but with the balanced, powerful offense Huffman has, we know we're going to have to go about 110 percent on every down. I picked Huffman to be No. 1 this year before the season started, and I still feel that way. I see no weaknesses."

Gerelds's concerns about the Vikings proved to be prophetic, as the Colonels struggled to do much of anything against Huffman until the fourth quarter. After falling behind 14–6, Woodlawn was in position to get back into the game. Hammock threw a bomb toward the end zone for tight end Scott Humphries, but the ball was deflected and intercepted by cornerback Don Saab. The play seemed to take the wind out of the Colonels' sails, and the Vikings easily drove for another touchdown to secure a 20–6 victory.

After suffering their first defeat of the season, Woodlawn bounced back for a 20–12 victory over West End High at Legion Field the next week. Ronnie Garzarek was the hero, after he picked off the ball on an option play and ran it back 65 yards for a touchdown in the third quarter. In the closing minutes, the Lions were driving for a chance to tie the game, but Nathan tipped a pass that was intercepted by Holland.

With a 5–1 record, the Colonels' playoff chances came down to their annual rivalry game against Banks High School at Legion Field on October 20. The Banks-Woodlawn game was annually the biggest contest in high school football in the city. The Jets were 7–0 and ranked No. 1 in the state. They'd outscored their opponents 207–42 and were averaging 29.6 points per game behind sophomore quarterback Jeff Rutledge.

"I hope it means as much to us, but the way we looked in practice Monday, I just don't know," Banks High coach George "Shorty" White told the *News* three days before the game. "It just didn't seem like Woodlawn's week. We've played a lot of good teams so far this season, and have been fortunate enough to beat them. But I hope our kids don't fall into the trap of thinking this is just another good team. It's Woodlawn, and that makes it a real game in an average year. This year isn't average. They're above average, and they'll play like it."

On a chilly night at Legion Field, the Colonels proved to be no match for the Jets. Banks High went ahead 7–0 on Rutledge's touchdown pass to Steve Grefseng on a fourth-and-14 play. After the Colonels were forced to punt, Jets tailback Johnny Gunnels scored to make it 14–0. Then Gunnels scored again early in the third quarter to give Banks High a 21–0 lead. Woodlawn finally scored on Hammock's 55-yard touchdown pass to split end Steven Washington, but it proved to be too little in a 27–6 loss. Gunnels and teammate Rodney Johnson combined to run for 208 yards, and Woodlawn's offense couldn't do enough to keep up.

Losing to Banks High seemed to completely deflate the Colonels, who lost two of their final three games to finish the 1972 season with a 6–4 record. It was a one-game improvement over the 5–5 finish in Gerelds's first season in 1971. But for Woodlawn High to join the ranks of the city's best high school teams, Gerelds knew his offense was going to have to be a lot better.

Fortunately, Gerelds had a solution. He was going to move Nathan to tailback the next season—if he could persuade "Chicken Big" and, more important, his mother, to do it.

CHAPTER EIGHT

1973 SEASON

When Wales Goebel spoke to the Colonels in the gymnasium on the third night of their preseason camp, he offered the players and coaches a few words of encouragement. After watching the Colonels practice three times a day during preseason camp, Tandy Gerelds knew he needed whatever help he could get. The Colonels were still racially divided, and their differences were preventing them from becoming a good team.

During three weeks of practice the previous spring, Gerelds moved star safety Tony Nathan to tailback, after having a long heart-to-heart conversation with his mother. Louise Nathan initially resisted the idea but eventually agreed to allow the position change because Gerelds promised to protect her son. "You coached him last season," Gerelds told her. "I'm going to coach him this year."

Louise Nathan wasn't the only person Gerelds had to win over. Woodlawn High's players immediately recognized that Nathan could be a dynamic running back. But a few of Woodlawn's white players weren't excited about the possibility of an African American becoming the star of the team. Gerelds altered his offense to feature Nathan's running abilities—ditching the Wing-T offense for the I-formation.

Nathan broke off long runs the first couple of times he touched the ball during spring practice. He effortlessly made would-be tacklers miss, and no one could slow him down. The white players also didn't like the fact that Nathan would be replacing a white player in the backfield. During his first few practices as a running back, some of Nathan's teammates refused to block for him. But then senior fullback Mike Allison, one of the team captains, spoke up.

A few of Woodlawn High's white players weren't excited about the possibility of an African American becoming the star of the team.

"Mike said we were a team, and needed to work together," Nathan said. "He was a senior and everybody listened to him."

However, Allison's speech proved to be nothing more than a Band-Aid. During the Colonels' preseason camp at Woodlawn High School, the white and black players were as divided as ever. Gerelds knew they would have to come together as one unit if they were going to be more competitive in 1973. That's why he agreed to allow Goebel, a complete stranger, to speak to his players on the third night of camp.

"They tell me that y'all are ranked dead last in the polls this year," Goebel told the players. "That means the experts think you're the worst team in the city. No matter what they say about you, if you go out there and practice and give everything you've got and play 110 percent and hold nothing back, God will bless you. I'm not saying you'll win every game or be successful on every play, but if you play for the glory of God and can look in the mirror after practice and say, 'I've given everything I have,' God will bless you."

After Goebel addressed the team, it wasn't long before Gerelds and his coaches started noticing changes in their players. Off the field, the white players were starting to socialize with the black players, and vice versa. Gerelds watched players of different races walking down the hallways of the school, laughing and joking with each other. Black players were sitting with their white teammates in the cafeteria. After most of the players answered Goebel's invitation to become Christians, racial boundaries began to blur.

"They started respecting each other and seeing each other as people, and not only football players and white kids and black kids," defensive coordinator Jerry Stearns said. "They became teammates and friends, and that bond between all of them was something special. They started going places together and were around each other more. Instead of the black kids being in one location and the white kids in another, they started interacting with each other. That led to them trusting each other. When you have kids who trust each other and like each other, it's going to make a difference in how they respond."

On the field, however, the Colonels still had plenty of issues to address. They weren't as bad as Goebel might have believed—in fact, they were considered a dark-horse candidate for a city championship—but there were still plenty of concerns about Woodlawn High's team heading into the '73 season.

The main concern was Nathan's health. He received quite a baptism during preseason camp. Nathan was one of the players who accepted Jesus Christ in the gym on that hot, muggy night, but he didn't exactly remember doing it. He had suffered a concussion earlier in the week and didn't remember much of anything after his mother dropped him off at the school for the start of the weeklong camp. On one of the first plays of the first scrimmage, Nathan was tackled and hit the back of his head. He returned to the huddle and ran the ball on the next play—and hit his head again. When the offense broke its huddle for the next play, Nathan just stood there.

"They said I had a great time at camp, but I don't remember it," Nathan said. "I remember my mom dropping me off, getting slammed to the ground, and then my mom picking me up. I lost a whole week of my life, which is a scary thing. I accepted Christ that night, but I don't remember it. I had to make that walk again."

Gerelds was concerned that his African American star would be a target for white players on other teams.

Because of lingering symptoms of the concussion, Nathan was kept out of contact drills for the final three weeks of preseason camp. Nathan had never played tailback in a game, and Gerelds was worried about him missing so much practice. Not only would Nathan's conditioning be hampered, but he would also miss valuable reps in getting used to running with the ball. Gerelds was also concerned that his African American star would be a target for other teams. Coach Gerelds knew there were probably plenty of white players on opposing teams who would love to have a shot at hitting Nathan, especially if he was as good as the coaches believed he would be. Allison and Peyton Zarzour had already been instructed to help protect Nathan on the field.

If opponents tried to take cheap shots or late hits, Allison and Zarzour were supposed to be there to protect him.

Nathan's health wasn't the only concern for the Colonels. Besides losing star defensive players Bubba Holland and Kirk Price, who were now freshmen at Auburn University and the University of Georgia, respectively, Woodlawn also had to replace departed starting quarterback Jimmy Hammock. Senior Ronald Mumm, who played sparingly the previous season, was the heir apparent. But Mumm didn't look like the answer early in preseason camp.

"This might be the worst team in Woodlawn High School history," Stearns said.

Gerelds and Stearns couldn't tell that to Hank Erwin, their new team chaplain, who was a tightly wound ball of energy and enthusiasm. He spent most of his time talking to the players about faith, while trying to convince them that they could accomplish anything if they devoted their lives to Jesus Christ and made an all-out commitment to serving Him. During a Fellowship of Christian Athletes meeting shortly after the 1973–74 school year started, Erwin issued a challenge to the players.

"Why don't you give your season to Christ and play for His glory and just see what happens?" Erwin said. "Who knows? It could be beyond your wildest imagination."

Much to Erwin's surprise, the players agreed and dedicated the season to glorifying God.

"It answered a prayer that I had been carrying with me for three or four years," Erwin said. "I saw what an improvement Christ made in me and then saw what it could do for a few members of my team when I was playing baseball at Troy State. I'd carried around a dream, wondering what would happen if an entire team committed to Christ. It was like the Lord was telling me, 'Here is your chance. You have an entire team committed to Christ. Let's see what happens.'"

The Colonels opened the season against Ensley High School at Legion Field on September 7. Woodlawn High's previous season ended with a 20–6 loss to the Yellow Jackets, and their opponent was supposed to be even better this year.

"We face probably the strongest team in the city on Friday night, and it will be a strong test for our players," Gerelds told *The Birmingham News*. "Ensley has nearly all of their starters back [and] are a predominantly senior club. We expect to field a fine team that will improve with experience."

After the Colonels went through their pregame warm-ups, Gerelds reluctantly allowed his new team chaplain to give a pregame speech to the players. Gerelds might have been more eager to allow it if Goebel had been there to make the address. Erwin was new to the ministry and Gerelds fondly called him "Rookie."

As the players and coaches gathered around Erwin in the locker room, he told them: "Bow your heads. Let's pray."

Then Erwin tightly clutched the newspaper he was holding in his hand.

"No, you know what? Before we pray I have something to say," Erwin said.

"Do we still bow our heads?" Stearns asked.

"No. Well, yes," Erwin said, as he stumbled for words. "First no, until I finish. Then yes."

"So right now?" Stearns asked.

"Not right now," Erwin said. "I'll tell you when, Jerry."

Erwin took a deep breath, gathered his thoughts, and then addressed the players.

"*The Birmingham News* believes something about this team.

They believe you'll only win two games; that this season is the death rattle of a school barely able to stay alive. They believe tonight will be an embarrassment. What about you? What do you believe?"

Now Erwin was pacing in the locker room and getting louder. He even tossed aside a baseball bat he was using to help him keep his balance on the leg he'd injured in college.

"You see, I believe your fate is not determined by some newspaper reporter any more than mine is by some doctor that told me I'd never walk again," Erwin said. "Because those people haven't seen what I've seen. They don't know what I know. I believe God honors those who honor Him. I don't know what's going to happen this year, but I believe it will be something we will remember for the rest of our lives. I believe it will be undeniable.

"What I'm asking you here today, right here,
right now is, will you believe with me?"

"I guess what I'm asking you here today, right here, right now is, will you believe with me?"

By the time Erwin was finished, the players were clapping in unison. It grew louder and louder as they lined up to take the field.

"Believe with me!" Erwin shouted.

The team members shouted back in unison, "We believe!" They continued to clap as they ran onto the field.

Gerelds's concerns about Nathan missing so much practice time came to fruition early in the game. The Colonels drove deep into Ensley territory on their opening drive, but Nathan fumbled and the Yellow Jackets recovered. Fortunately, a holding penalty wiped out an Ensley touchdown run, and then Woodlawn's defense held on fourth down. In the second quarter, the Yellow Jackets had the ball at the Colonels' three-yard line. On fourth down, though, Allison charged into the backfield and threw the ball carrier for a nine-yard loss. It was a scoreless tie at the half.

Even though Woodlawn's offense struggled to move the ball, like it had during much of the previous season, the Colonels were excited about how they'd played in the first half. Erwin was even more excited. He'd paced the sideline for two quarters as he tried to figure out what he'd say to the players at halftime.

"This is a little indication of what God can do," Erwin told them. "But remember—it's not you. It's God showing you what He can do through you."

In the third quarter, Nathan returned a punt 42 yards to set up Buzz Walsh's 29-yard field goal, which gave the Colonels a 3–0 lead. The Yellow Jackets were seemingly moving the ball at will on offense, but Woodlawn's defense bowed its neck when it needed to most. The Colonels recovered a fumble in the third quarter and then intercepted a pass in the fourth.

Trailing 3–0 late in the game, Ensley took possession with just under four minutes left. The Yellow Jackets started their final drive at their 25-yard line, and then marched 75 yards in 13 plays. Quarterback David McKinney scored on a two-yard run with one minute, 52 seconds left to give Ensley a 7–3 victory. It was a bittersweet defeat for the Colonels in their opener. The Colonels didn't do much of anything to alleviate Gerelds's concerns about his offense; they picked up only seven first downs (just one in the second half) and finished with 149 yards of offense.

LEFT: A very young Tandy Gerelds with his father, Tommy Fraser Gerelds.

BELOW: Tandy Gerelds launches a home run for Auburn versus Florida State as a senior in 1964. Auburn won the SEC baseball championship during his junior season.

LEFT: Coach Tandy Gerelds in his first season as Woodlawn High School's football coach. He was only 29 years old.

ABOVE: Debbie Johnson (second from right) was one of Woodlawn High School's cheerleaders in 1963. She later became Tandy Gerelds's wife.

1966, Tandy and Debbie Gerelds. (Pregnant with first daughter, Jessica).

Coach Gerelds making a funny face after David Langner most assuredly said something crazy.

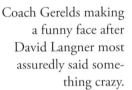

ABOVE: Sophomore safety Tony Nathan (42) makes a play in pass coverage at Woodlawn High School in 1972. Nathan changed his jersey number the next season.

RIGHT: Tony Nathan (22) breaking away for a long run during a game in 1973. Fullback Mike Allison (30) was one of his lead blockers.

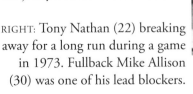

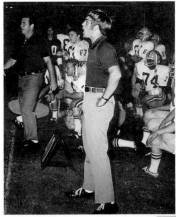

Assistant coach Jimmy Williams with Coach Tandy Gerelds (top left) on the sideline during the 1973-74 season.

Coach Gerelds listening to Woodlawn quarterback Ronald Mumm in 1973. Mumm was later the commander of the U.S. Air Force Thunderbirds.

LEFT: The 1973 Woodlawn High School coaching staff: James Rancont (left), Jerry Stearns (middle), Jimmy Williams (right) and Tandy Gerelds (kneeling).

RIGHT: Coach Gerelds speaking at the 1973-74 Woodlawn High School athletics banquet.

LEFT: Coach Gerelds, with 1974 all-state linebacker Rocha McKinstry and his mother, as McKinstry accepted a scholarship from Auburn University.

RIGHT: Running back Tony Nathan receiving an award from Coach Gerelds at the 1973-74 Woodlawn High School athletics banquet.

LEFT: Coach Gerelds, Tony Nathan, and legendary Auburn University coach Ralph "Shug" Jordan at the Woodlawn High School athletics banquet.

RIGHT: Coach Gerelds with Peyton Zarzour, Legion Field, 1974.

ABOVE: Coach Gerelds speaking to the student body at a pep rally at Woodlawn, 1974.

RIGHT: Coach Gerelds on the Woodlawn sideline.

LEFT: Hank Erwin and his wife, Sheila, met while they were students at Troy State University in Troy, Alabama. Hank served as Woodlawn High School's team chaplain during the early 1970s and later became an Alabama state senator.

RIGHT: Evangelist Wales Goebel addressed the Woodlawn High School Colonels before the 1973 season. He served many high schools throughout the southeast.

LEFT: Coach Gerelds escorted his daughter Jessica when she was named homecoming queen at Hewitt Trussville High School in 1983.

RIGHT: "Touchdown" Tony Nathan turns the corner into the open field.

LEFT: Todd Gerelds (the author of this book) played for his father at Deshler High School in Tuscumbia, Alabama, during the mid 1980s.

RIGHT: Todd Gerelds tries to break away for a long run versus Muscle Shoals High School in 1985.

LEFT: Coach Gerelds and his wife Debbie joined their daughter Jill on the field during Deshler High School's senior night in 1989.

BELOW: Coach Gerelds addresses his players at Deshler High School during the 1988-89 season. He coached the Tigers for eleven seasons, making the state playoffs each year.

ABOVE: The 1990 Deshler High Scool team finished 15–0 and won the Alabama Class 4A state championship.

LEFT: Coach Gerelds's final season on the sideline was at Belmont High School in Belmont, Mississippi, in 2002. He was diagnosed with cancer only days before the start of summer practice. His coaching staff there (left to right): Kevin Deaton, Glenn Elmore, Tandy Gerelds, Kerry Moody.

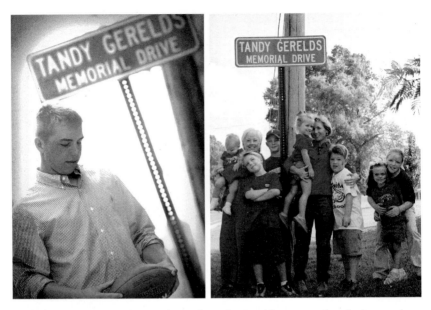

LEFT: Tucker Norwood, grandson of Tandy Gerelds, pictured with the sign memorializing Coach Gerelds's route to Deshler High School. The city of Tuscumbia designated Woodmont Drive that runs through town up to the school: Tandy Gerelds Memorial Drive.

RIGHT: Left to right: Debbie Gerelds (holding granddaughter Allison Gerelds), Tucker Norwood, Ben Norwood, Jessica Norwood (holding son Bailey Kay Gerelds), Jacob Norwood, Morgan Gerelds, and Molly Norwood.

LEFT: Coach Tandy Gerelds and Debbie Gerelds's children: Jill Gerelds Christopher, Todd Gerelds, and Jessica Gerelds Norwood.

RIGHT: Former Woodlawn High School teammates, Reginald Green and Tony Nathan, with Todd Gerelds on the movie set for Woodlawn in 2014.

Once the Colonels loaded the bus to make the short drive back to Woodlawn High School, Erwin climbed into a front seat with Gerelds. The players were quiet in the locker room after the game, and now Erwin could hear a pin drop on the bus. "You better say something to them," Gerelds said. "Their hopes and dreams have been crushed."

Erwin took a couple of minutes to gather his thoughts and muster the courage to address the dejected players. Then he stood up and looked down the dark, quiet bus.

"Now, fellas, I want you to understand that with every commitment to Christ there is a test to find out whether you are trying to use Jesus as a rabbit's foot or a lucky charm, or whether you really mean what you say—that you'll play for the glory of God regardless of the outcome," Erwin said. "This is a test to see your real motive. Did you really want Christ to be glorified, whether you won or lost, or were you using Him as a rabbit's foot or lucky charm? He has to be the Lord of all Lords. Are you totally bought in?"

From the back of the bus, Erwin heard somebody shout, "I'm bought in." Someone else said it and then another. Within a few minutes, the entire mood on the bus changed. Dejection and sadness were replaced by excitement and energy.

"Although we suffered a loss, we saw such a transformation that we knew we were going to win some games and possibly even win a championship," offensive lineman Reginald Greene said. "After that game, everybody got better and better."

Before a practice the next week, Erwin found Nathan sitting in the stands of the stadium alone. Erwin figured it was a good time to talk to the quiet and reluctant star in the making.

"Tony, I don't talk like Wales," Erwin said. "I don't give the big speeches. I have something I've wanted to say to you since the first time I saw you run. There's something special about you, Tony. It's something that can't be taught. It can only be given. And you have to decide what to do with it. Now, when you play for yourself, you can be great. But when you play for a purpose higher than yourself, well, that's when extraordinary things can happen. God has a plan for your life that isn't insignificant. I can't know, of course, but I believe He wants you to be a superstar."

Nathan looked at Erwin and didn't know what to say. Even at sixteen, Nathan was old enough to know that Birmingham wasn't ready for an African American superstar. And it wasn't like he'd shown that much promise in the first game. Ensley High's defense had done an efficient job of containing Nathan, holding him to 57 yards on 14 carries with no touchdowns.

"I'm going to tell you a secret, and I guarantee you that if you do this, you'll be a superstar in two years," Erwin said.

"What is it?" Nathan asked.

"If you do those three things, I guarantee
you'll be a superstar."

"One, live your life totally to serve the Lord and give Him 110 percent every day," Erwin said. "You walk the talk and ask Christ to be your Savior and Lord of your life. You walk the talk in school, at home, and in your community. Two, you give 110 percent every day on this practice field. There can't be any slacking off, and learn your position. Thirdly, when you play, you give it everything you have and leave only sweat on the field. If you do those three things, I guarantee you'll be a superstar."

After a short prayer together, Nathan left to join his teammates in the locker room to dress for practice, while keeping
what Erwin said to him in the back of his mind. Nathan started
to show more promise the following week against Hayes High,
which was the school he would have attended if Birmingham's
high schools hadn't been integrated. Nathan ran for two touchdowns against the Pacesetters, helping the Colonels win their first
game of the season by a 14–3 score. It was a much better performance, but Coach Gerelds certainly couldn't have imagined what
was coming next.

On September 21, Woodlawn High played Vestavia Hills
High at Lawson Field. The Rebels had won two of their first three
games, shutting out Glenn High and Ramsay High by a combined score of 42–0 and losing to Mountain Brook by only one
point, 17–16. But Vestavia Hills wasn't ready for what they faced
against the Colonels. Woodlawn took a 14–7 lead at the half,
and then Nathan scored three times in a six-minute, six-second
span in the third quarter. He scored on a 90-yard kickoff return,
a 19-yard run around right end, and then a 77-yard burst up the
middle. By the time Nathan went to the bench with about six
minutes left in the third quarter, he had amassed 410 all-purpose
yards—227 rushing, 113 on two kickoff returns, 58 on three
punt returns, and 12 on a halfback pass for a touchdown. What
was even more impressive was that he'd only touched the ball 20
times in the game and scored four touchdowns.

"I've never seen anything like it on a team of mine," Gerelds
told *The Birmingham News* after the 41–14 victory.

The next week against Erwin High School, Nathan ran for
203 yards and scored two touchdowns in a 21–6 victory. He'd
scored six touchdowns in two games, and football fans in Bir-

mingham and across the state were starting to take notice of him—and the Colonels.

"They said we were one-dimensional," quarterback Denny Ragland said. "That wasn't actually true because we had two dimensions—Tony left and Tony right."

After the 3–1 start, excitement and faith were starting to build at Woodlawn High School. Erwin was leading weekly Bible studies for the players, and Woodlawn Baptist Church, which was next to the school, hosted a Friday morning prayer breakfast on game days. Goebel or another preacher opened the 6 a.m. breakfasts with a devotional, and the event soon attracted other students, not just the football players. Woodlawn's cheerleaders started writing Bible verses on the banners that players ran through when they took the field, and players wrote Scripture on tape that was attached to the back of their helmets and on their shoes.

"Everybody was starting to ask, 'What's going on at Woodlawn?'" Erwin said. "No one could explain it."

Now the Colonels had to prepare to play Huffman High School, which was the No. 1–ranked team in the state in Class 4A. Woodlawn High hadn't defeated the Vikings in three years, and had lost to them 20–6 the previous season. The Vikings had a big runner in Steve Whitman, who would later become a bruising fullback at the University of Alabama, and a speedy runner in Allen Crumbley, who would become a shutdown cornerback for the Crimson Tide. The Vikings were 5–0 after narrowly defeating Jeff Davis High of Montgomery 21–20 in their previous game.

When Erwin wandered into the coaches' offices at Woodlawn on the day before the game, Gerelds and his assistants weren't in a very good mood.

"They told me it was going to be terrible," Erwin said. "They watched Huffman on film and said we were going to get crushed. They told me they were monsters. I heard all of that, but I knew what the Lord could do in spite of it."

As Erwin left their offices, he wondered what he would say to the Woodlawn High players to convince them they could actually compete with what seemed to be an insurmountable opponent.

"I did something that I'd never done before," Erwin said.

Erwin planned to do the only thing that came to his mind—he was going to pray to God for a victory.

"Some could criticize it with, 'Oh, give me a break,'" Erwin said. "But you have to understand that I had only been a Christian for about four years and had a young faith. I took things literally and with common sense, but also with a daringness that I should be able to talk to Him as a Father because I was His son. I thought I should be able to ask Him for things. If you need something, ask Him for it. That's what prayer is all about, right?"

Following the prayer breakfast on Friday morning, Erwin remained at Woodlawn Baptist Church and prayed.

"Now, God, these kids have devoted this season to glorifying Your name and they have been faithful to uplift You in these past games in a remarkable way," Erwin poured out his heart to God, expressing his concerns for the fragile young faith that was growing in these new believers. He asked God to show them that even when the foe was seemingly invincible nothing was impossible with Him.

He prayed, "Lord, can You do something special? Can You prove to these boys that it's not by power or might, but it's with Your name that victory can be achieved? Will You give them the

game? I know You can control a game, just like you can control
the sun or the moon or the waves of the sea. A little ole football
game is nothing compared to that. Would You do a special favor?
Will You give them the game so that they can see that You can
defeat the largest giant?"

After finishing the prayer, Erwin opened his Bible as he usually did after praying. Remarkably, he came to 1 Samuel 17,
verses 43–50. It was the story of David versus Goliath:

> *He said to David, "Am I a dog, that you come at me with sticks?"*
> *And the Philistine cursed David by his gods. "Come here," he said,*
> *"and I'll give your flesh to the birds and the wild animals!"*
>
> *David said to the Philistine, "You come against me with sword*
> *and spear and javelin, but I come against you in the name of the*
> *Lord Almighty, the God of the armies of Israel, whom you have*
> *defied. This day the Lord will deliver you into my hands, and I'll*
> *strike you down and cut off your head. This very day I will give the*
> *carcasses of the Philistine army to the birds and the wild animals,*
> *and the whole world will know that there is a God in Israel. All*
> *those gathered here will know that it is not by sword or spear that*
> *the Lord saves; for the battle is the Lord's, and he will give all of you*
> *into our hands."*
>
> *As the Philistine moved closer to attack him, David ran quickly*
> *toward the battle line to meet him. Reaching into his bag and tak-*
> *ing out a stone, he slung it and struck the Philistine on the fore-*
> *head. The stone sank into his forehead, and he fell facedown on the*
> *ground.*
>
> *So David triumphed over the Philistine with a sling and a*
> *stone; without a sword in his hand he struck down the Philistine*
> *and killed him.*

The Scripture hit Erwin like a runaway truck.

"If you ever want to say that God jumped out at you through the pages and was speaking to you, this was it," Erwin said. "David wasn't going to win because of his size or because he could throw a rock. He was going to win so the world would know there is a God in Israel. That's how he was going to win. That jumped off the page at me."

"Whoa," Erwin thought to himself. "We're going to win this thing!"

"Whoa," Erwin thought to himself.
"We're going to win this thing!"

Erwin returned to the coaches' offices at three that afternoon, and they were even more depressed after watching film of the Huffman High team again.

"We're going to get clobbered," Stearns said. "We're going to get killed."

"No, you're not," Erwin said. "God has shown me that we're going to win."

"What planet are you from?" Gerelds asked.

"Get your Bibles out and turn to 1 Samuel 17," Erwin said. "I've got some errands to run, but I'm coming back. I will test you on it."

When Erwin returned, there was a completely different atmosphere inside the coaches' offices. Once the Woodlawn team loaded the buses to go to Lawson Field to play the Vikings, Erwin read the players the same Scripture. They were soon bouncing in their seats with excitement and confidence. When the players took the field for warm-ups, however, they realized the Vikings actually did look a lot like Goliath.

"They got quieter and quieter," Erwin said. "They saw the enemy and knew we were in trouble."

"Don't worry about them," Erwin said, as he tried to reassure the Colonels. "You're going to win this game!"

Huffman took the opening kickoff and drove 60 yards for a touchdown in 11 plays. Quarterback Gary Woods threw a touchdown to David Denton, but the Vikings missed the point-after kick for a 6–0 lead. On the sideline, Gerelds gave Erwin a long look and shook his head. Erwin couldn't do anything but give him a thumbs-up.

On the Colonels' ensuing possession, they faced fourth-and-one at Huffman High's 31-yard line. Mumm took the snap and pitched the ball to Nathan. Mike Allison sealed off the defensive end, and Nathan broke inside and then back outside. He reached the sideline and ran 31 yards for a touchdown. Buzzy Walsh kicked the extra point for a 7–6 lead, and Woodlawn High never looked back.

Bobby Thompson intercepted a pass on Huffman's next possession, and Nathan ran for a 14-yard touchdown on another fourth-and-one play to make it 14–6. Then Woodlawn's Tommy Conwell intercepted a pass and returned it 27 yards for a touchdown for a 20–6 lead at the half. The Vikings scored early in the second half to make it 20–12, but then Nathan ran for two more touchdowns to give the Colonels a 35–12 victory. Nathan finished the game with 231 rushing yards and scored four touchdowns and a two-point conversion.

As the final seconds ticked off the clock, Allison found Erwin on the sideline. Tears were streaming down Allison's face.

"I've never seen anything like this in my life," Allison said. "This is crazy."

David slayed Goliath. Even Gerelds must have believed it was divine intervention.

"I give full credit to winning this game to Jesus Christ," Gerelds told the *Birmingham Post-Herald* after the game. "Tony Nathan is a different football player after becoming a Christian, and I'm happy to say all my 36 football players are Christians. We dedicated this game to Christ, and that's the reason we won."

"We dedicated this game to Christ, and
that's the reason we won."

Once the players gathered in the locker room after their improbable victory, Erwin delivered a postgame prayer: "Lord, You have shown that it's not by power or might that you win, but it's by the power of the Lord that you win against a great giant. You've proven tonight that there is a God in Israel."

When the team gathered in Woodlawn High's cafeteria the next Monday night to watch film of its victory, Gerelds showed them a replay of one of Nathan's long punt returns. Every Woodlawn player correctly made his block. Brad Hendrix and Jay Blackwood even knocked their defenders off their feet and out of the game with injuries. Gerelds showed the play to his team over and over again.

"It's the first time in my career that I've seen a perfect play," Gerelds told them. "Every man blocked somebody. It was perfect."

The following week, Al O'Brien of *The Birmingham News* christened Nathan with the nickname "Travelin' Tony."

"Tony Nathan took a series of Sherman-like marches through Lawson Field Friday night, leaving a bruised heap of Vikings in his delicately destructive wake and a glassy-eyed, head-shaking and open-mouthed audience to tell the story," O'Brien wrote. "The Woodlawn foot magician, his speed and moves big league stuff from first to last, gained 231 of his team's 267 total yards in a 35–12 painful spanking of top-ranked and powerful Huffman, and superlatives that had been in abeyance for years fell like torrential rain. Believers are everywhere. The close to incredible performance, which included four touchdowns and one two-point conversion, culminated a fantastic fortnight for 'Travelin' Tony.'"

O'Brien went as far as calling Nathan the best high school running back in Birmingham in several years, "surpassing even Banks's great Johnny Musso, later a University of Alabama All-American." But the "Travelin' Tony" nickname didn't stick, as Nathan's teammates and classmates preferred calling him "Touchdown Tony."

The attention and accolades were unfamiliar territory for Nathan, who was quickly becoming one of the most prized college football recruits in the country. When the Birmingham Touchdown Club honored Nathan as its Player of the Week for his performance against Huffman High, North Carolina State coach Lou Holtz was the featured speaker and made sure he introduced himself to Nathan and his parents. *The Birmingham News* even speculated that the most heated recruiting battle for Nathan might be between Alabama football coach Paul "Bear" Bryant and Crimson Tide basketball coach C. M. Newton, who both wanted Nathan to play their sport in college. Nathan went out of his way to acknowledge and thank his teammates and coaches whenever he was honored.

Nathan went out of his way to acknowledge and thank his teammates and coaches whenever he was honored.

"Tony was a great, great kid," Stearns said. "I don't think he let the notoriety bother him in any way. I don't ever remember him thinking that he was better than any of the other kids. He always gave credit to his teammates. He was just a pleasure to be around."

Nathan's parents worked hard to teach him humility, and they made sure he didn't think he was better than anyone else, especially his brothers and sisters, even as he became a household name in Birmingham and other parts of the state. When Gerelds arrived at the Nathan home to pick up Tony so he could be honored at another Birmingham Touchdown Club meeting, he had to wait until Nathan finished washing dishes. "Touchdown Tony" still had to complete his chores.

After upsetting the No. 1–ranked team in the state, the Colonels had to play No. 2 West End High the next week. There was no rest for the weary. Gerelds knew upsetting the Vikings had taken a toll on his team, and he worried that his players might not be able to bounce back quickly—both mentally and physically.

"West End has the best personnel they've had over there in quite some time," Gerelds told the *Birmingham Post-Herald* a few days before the game. "They're big and quick, and they're well coached. It seems like the entire defensive team is agile. No doubt the key to victory will be moving the ball against them."

The Colonels answered the bell against West End High at Lawson Field on October 12, taking the opening kickoff and driving for a touchdown. Nathan scored on a nine-yard run, and Walsh kicked the extra point for a 7–0 lead. As Gerelds expected, it was a black-and-blue game. The Colonels had problems moving the ball against the Lions and didn't score the rest of the first half. In the closing seconds of the half, West End's Tony Hendon intercepted Ronald Mumm's pass and returned it to the Woodlawn 16 with only two seconds remaining. On the final play of the half, Lions quarterback Mark Kreider threw a two-yard touchdown to Harold Wells in the corner of the end zone. But the Colonels were able to hold a 7–6 lead because linebacker Tommy Rue blocked West End's point-after kick.

In the third quarter, the Lions recovered a fumble and then drove 55 yards for a touchdown, with Aaron Dorsey scoring on a four-yard run. West End failed on a two-point conversion pass, leaving it with a 12–7 lead. That's where the score remained until late in the fourth quarter. The Colonels took possession at their 25-yard line with about five minutes to go, and then they started feeding the ball to their workhorse. Nathan ran for 80 yards on the drive, including a 29-yard touchdown that gave the Colonels a 13–12 lead. After forcing the Lions to turn the ball over on downs, Woodlawn High upset an undefeated team for the second week in a row.

"All I can say, and I mean it sincerely, is that God has been mighty good to me and these boys," Gerelds told *The Birmingham News*.

After accomplishing so much the previous two weeks, the Colonels still faced one huge obstacle in their quest for the playoffs—Banks High School. The Jets were Woodlawn High's arch-nemesis. Banks High was the defending Class 4A state champion, after going 12–0–1 in 1972. After finishing the 1972 regular season with a 14–14 tie against Berry High School in the Clinic Game at Legion Field, the Jets won three straight in the state playoffs, including a 34–8 victory over Huffman in the championship game.

Banks High junior Jeff Rutledge was one of the best high school quarterbacks in the country, and he had plenty of help around him. The Jets had three menacing defensive ends—Bob Grefseng, Freddie Knighton, and Joe Shaw—who were capable of making Mumm's night miserable. Knighton would sign with Alabama after the season, Shaw would attend Auburn, and Grefseng would play at Ole Miss. The Jets won their first six games in 1973 and hadn't tasted defeat since losing to Woodlawn 21–18 at the end of the 1971 season.

At the start of the game at Legion Field on October 19, Nathan still looked like the best player on the field. Woodlawn took the opening kickoff and needed only four plays to score a touchdown, with Nathan running 33 yards into the end zone for a 7–0 lead. But that was all the scoring the Jets would surrender in a 17–7 victory. Banks High's defense held Nathan to 124 yards on 31 carries, including only 26 yards in the second half. Jets tailbacks Jerry Murphree and Joel Wahl combined to run for 207 yards, and Rutledge completed five of eight passes for 80 yards. Once again, the Jets had the Colonels' number.

The next week, Thompson intercepted four passes in Woodlawn's 29–6 win over Parker High School. Nathan got back on track, running for 177 yards with three touchdowns. But then Nathan broke his foot in the first half against Phillips High on November 1. "With Nathan on the sideline," *The Birmingham News* reported, "the Colonel offense was like a fuse with no bomb attached." After Phillips went ahead 13–6 on Fred Robinson's eight-yard touchdown in the third quarter, Woodlawn's hopes of winning seemed over. With time running out, Buzzy Walsh, the backup quarterback, fired a 37-yard bomb to Mike Grauel to put the Colonels in position to win. Backup tailback Bill White scored on a one-yard run to cut Phillips High's lead to 13–12, and then Gerelds decided to go for a two-point conversion and a victory. Mumm, who had proved to be a more than capable quarterback over the course of the season, threw a two-point pass to Howard Ross, giving the Colonels an unlikely 14–13 victory. By the time the Colonels played their last regular season game, against Ramsay High, on November 8, seven starters were sidelined with injuries, including Nathan. The injuries piled up so quickly that Woodlawn's players became superstitious.

"There was a whole row of crutches on the sideline," Reginald Greene said. "Somebody said, 'Don't touch the crutch or you'll be the next one to get hurt.'"

The injuries piled up so quickly that Woodlawn's players became superstitious.

Playing mostly backups, the Colonels defeated Ramsay High 14–0 to finish the season with an 8–2 record. Woodlawn High ultimately fell short of its goal of making the playoffs—Banks

High would finish 13–0 and win a second straight Class 4A state championship—but it was a season the Colonels would never forget. And there were plenty of reasons to be excited about the 1974 season, when most of the team's best players would be seniors.

"We defied the newspaper pundits and logic through the power of the Lord," Erwin said. "We made an amazing statement that anything was possible if you dedicate yourself to the Lord. I got a chance to see the answer to my dream of seeing what could happen when an entire team dedicated their lives to Christ and played for His glory. To see that, yes, it can be done and remarkable magic can happen on the football field, not by some kind of sorcery but by the power of God. The 1973 season will always be the year that I saw God come down and play football in Birmingham."

CHAPTER NINE

1974 SEASON

People from Alabama like to say that you have to select a favorite college football team from your mother's womb. It's almost as if you have to choose between the University of Alabama and Auburn University as soon as you take your first breath. The state seems to be divided right down the middle, with half of the population cheering for the Crimson Tide and the other half rooting for the Tigers. The fanaticism and state bragging rights are a big reason the Alabama-Auburn game might be the most heated and anticipated rivalry in the country every season. The Iron Bowl between Alabama and Auburn might be the only game that's talked about 365 days of every year.

In Alabama high school football, there wasn't a better rivalry than Woodlawn High School versus Banks High School. The schools were only separated by a four-mile drive down 1st Avenue North. Woodlawn High is located in the Woodlawn neighborhood, on the south side of Interstate 20 and is closer to downtown Birmingham. Banks High School occupied six buildings on 86th Street South in the South East Lake neighborhood, which is on the north side of I-20.

Woodlawn is a much older school, first opening the doors to its permanent school in 1922. The Colonels have a proud football tradition, winning state championships in 1937, 1941, 1942, 1943, 1955, and 1956. Woodlawn High produced the likes of Alabama All-American Harry Gilmer (class of 1943) and legendary Florida State University coach Bobby Bowden (class of 1948).

Woodlawn High produced Alabama All-American Harry Gilmer and legendary Florida State University coach Bobby Bowden.

Banks High School didn't open until 1957, accepting only freshmen the first year, and thus didn't have its first graduating class until 1961. During the 1960–61 school year, the Jets swept city championships in baseball, boys' basketball, and football. The Jets won football state championships in 1965, 1972, and 1973. Alabama All-American running back Johnny "Italian Stallion" Musso played at Banks High, as well as Auburn quarterback Jimmy Sidle and David Cutcliffe, who would become a head coach at Ole Miss and Duke University.

While Woodlawn High students and alumni liked to think their school was the most storied in the city, Banks High wasn't afraid to step on its toes as the new kid on the block. To put it politely, the Colonels and Jets didn't like each other very much.

"If you were a Woodlawn person, you really disliked Banks," said Debbie Gerelds, the wife of Coach Gerelds. "Woodlawn was the main school in the eastern part of Birmingham. Banks was still a relatively new school. They infringed on our territory."

The football rivalry between the schools was even more intense because players from both teams were so familiar with each other. They had been teammates on youth football teams that played at Crestwood Park, East Lake Park, and Wahouma Park. They had attended the same grammar schools and went to church together. Banks High School players dated girls from Woodlawn High, and vice versa. Some families were split down the middle—Woodlawn quarterback Denny Ragland's sisters attended Banks.

Colonels defensive coordinator Jerry Stearns remembered his first experience in the Woodlawn-Banks rivalry. A few days before the 1971 game, he heard Woodlawn students slamming lunch trays in the cafeteria and chanting, "Rip Jets! Rip Jets! Rip those Sugar Jets!" Woodlawn students liked to call the Jets the "Sugar Jets," which was a popular breakfast cereal at the time (Banks students liked to counter with "Pop Those Colonels!").

"Are we going to stop this?" Stearns asked Gerelds, as the lunch trays got louder and louder.

"Nah, it's just Woodlawn versus Banks week," Gerelds told him.

Woodlawn High students also liked to pull an annual prank by painting the U.S. Air Force F-86D Sabre fighter jet that was a landmark on the roof of Banks High School. The Korean War–era jet, which was loaned to the school by the Alabama Air National Guard, was painted Banks's school colors of Columbia blue and scarlet. Every year, it seemed, the jet would somehow be repainted in Woodlawn High's school colors of green and gold.

"Painting that jet was a victory in itself," Colonels offensive lineman Reginald Greene said.

The Colonels had even more reason to dislike Banks High School in the early '70s—they couldn't seem to beat the Jets. After defeating Banks High at the end of the '71 season, the Colonels lost to the Jets in each of the next three seasons. Because both teams played in the same region in Class 4A, which was the largest classification in Alabama at the time, only one of them could advance to the state playoffs. After losing to the Jets in 1972 and 1973, the Colonels had to watch their archrivals win back-to-back state championships. It was a tough pill to swallow.

"There was no love lost between Banks and Woodlawn," Stearns said. "It was the craziest thing I'd ever seen. Every other week of the school year, the kids got along fine. But then it was like the Battle of 1st Avenue North. People think the Auburn-Alabama rivalry is intense. Banks versus Woodlawn was just as intense."

By the start of the 1974 season, the rivalry between the two high schools had cooled a bit—it was more like post–Cold War. The previous spring, a handful of Woodlawn High players, including tailback Tony Nathan, fullback Mike Allison, and linebacker Peyton Zarzour, asked team chaplain Hank Erwin to arrange for them to speak to Banks High's players about their commitment to Christ and how God had changed their lives. As the Woodlawn High players became stronger in their faith, they realized it was their duty to share the Gospel with others. They had learned that Matthew 28:18–20 says, "Then Jesus came to them and said, 'All authority in heaven and on earth has been given to me. Therefore go and make disciples of all nations, baptizing them in the name of the Father and of the Son and of the Holy Spirit, and teaching them to obey everything I have commanded you. And surely I am with you always, to the very end of the age.' "

"It was remarkable to even take this step because Woodlawn and Banks didn't like each other," Erwin said. "They were so competitive and there was an intense rivalry."

Erwin arranged for the Woodlawn High and Banks High players to meet at Cascade Plunge, which was a popular swimming pool in East Lake. It might have been the coldest swimming hole in the entire state because the pool was fed by a natural spring. It was the perfect place to cool off during sweltering Alabama summers.

When Erwin arrived at Cascade Plunge, he was surprised to see so many players from both schools there. Standing in the middle of their rivals, Nathan, Allison, Zarzour, and others talked to the Banks High players about their commitment to Christ and how it was the secret to their unexpected success in '73. The Woodlawn High players challenged the Jets to dedicate their season to Christ in '74.

"They sat there in stunned silence," Erwin said. "They didn't know what we were there to talk about."

Jets quarterback Jeff Rutledge, who along with Nathan was one of the most highly recruited college football prospects in the country, was impressed by what he heard. The Woodlawn High players talked about how their meeting with Goebel had changed their lives. Rutledge called Goebel a few days later and asked him to come talk to the Jets. But then Banks High's team chaplain called Goebel and told him that Jets coach George "Shorty" White wouldn't allow him to talk to his players.

"Shorty said he didn't want me or anyone else coming and preaching to his boys," Goebel said. "He only wanted them worried about football."

Rutledge was determined to have his teammates hear Goebel's message, so he arranged for the evangelist to speak to the team at a Baptist church. When Goebel arrived, White let him know that he wasn't happy about him being there.

"Jeff told Shorty I was their guest," Goebel said. "He made me feel very welcome."

As Goebel shared the same message he had given the Woodlawn High team a year earlier, he invited the Banks High players to ask Jesus Christ into their hearts and make Him their personal Lord and Savior. One of the first people to accept the invitation to become a Christian was Coach White. Erwin, who was also in the church that night, had witnessed Coach Gerelds's transformation the previous season. He hoped Christ would have a similar effect on White.

"Tandy was baptized and wanted his athletes to hear the story of Christ for the rest of his career," Erwin said. "He saw what happened to his players and yearned for that change. He wasn't going to push it on them, but he wanted every athlete who came through his program to have the opportunity to hear about Christ. He became fabulously respected for the goodness he gave to his players.

"When he gave his life to Christ, his whole personality about coaching changed. He started to love his players and care for his players. His players learned to love him. He got more out of his athletes than anyone I'd seen. They wanted to play for him. They played for him because they loved him."

"When [Gerelds] gave his life to Christ, his whole personality about coaching changed. He started to love and care for his players."

Banks and Woodlawn were considered the favorites to win the city championship in 1974, and the Jets were looking to win their third consecutive Class 4A state title. The Colonels were their biggest challenger, largely because Nathan was coming back. Even though many of Woodlawn's best players were now seniors, they would also have ten new starters in their lineup.

At the start of preseason practices, Reginald Greene noticed some changes in his team. Everyone seemed to be bigger and stronger. Rocha McKinstry, who didn't play football as a junior, was a budding 250-pound star linebacker. Lineman Jim Keeble was six-foot-four and weighed 260 pounds, which was considered really big in the early '70s. Even Greene, who admittedly was out of shape as a junior, had grown from 175 pounds to 215.

"God changed my taste buds," Greene said. "I started eating vegetables."

Woodlawn High opened the season against Ensley High at Legion Field on September 6. Much like in the previous season, the Colonels relied heavily on Nathan, who carried the ball twenty-one times for 266 yards with five touchdowns in a 35–21 victory over the Yellow Jackets. But Nathan was hurt on his final carry of the game, spraining his ankle with about one minute to go in the third quarter. Without Nathan on the field, sophomore fullback Dennis Rogers stepped in and ran thirteen times for 68 yards. Nathan's injury cast a big cloud over Woodlawn's first victory of the season.

"We won't know how bad it is until tomorrow," Gerelds told *The Birmingham News* after the game.

Fortunately for the Colonels, it was only a minor ankle injury. Nathan was able to play against Hayes High School the following Thursday night, although Gerelds used him sparingly in an easy 33–0 victory. After Nathan carried four times for 38 yards with two touchdowns in the first 14 minutes, Woodlawn's other running backs took over. The highlight of the contest might have been defensive end Brad Hendrix's punting. In a practice the previous week, Gerelds was so frustrated by his inconsistent punters that he threw up his hands and screamed, "Can anybody around here punt the ball?"

Hendrix, who was nicknamed "Gomer Pyle" by his teammates because of his closely cropped crew cut and resemblance to actor Jim Nabors, said he'd give it a try and boomed a 50-yard punt on his first attempt. Then he punted the ball 60 yards. After shanking a nine-yard punt on his first attempt against Hayes, Hendrix had punts of 55 and 40 yards. Hendrix's punting wasn't the only pleasant surprise. McKinstry was becoming the leader of Woodlawn High's defense, intercepting a pass and recovering a fumble against the Pacesetters.

"He has really made himself into a good football player and won the confidence of his teammates," Gerelds told the *Birmingham Post-Herald*. "He is one of the most improved players on the squad. He has gotten himself real quick, and fairly strong. I'm pleased with his progress."

Even after a 2–0 start, Gerelds was beginning to realize that his '74 team probably wasn't as good as the previous one. Nathan and his classmates were seniors, but the Colonels had lost some important pieces from 1973, including quarterback Ronald Mumm and Mike Allison, who had been Nathan's lead blocker. Even with Nathan in the backfield, Gerelds knew his team would have to win close ball games—and have a little bit of luck—if it was going to contend for a city championship and have a chance at making the state playoffs, which had eluded the team during the previous two seasons.

Opponents were going to do everything they could to slow

down Nathan. Against Phillips High School on September 20, the Red Raiders limited Nathan to only 26 yards on 10 carries in the first half. With Woodlawn's offense sputtering, the game was a scoreless tie at intermission. But then Nathan scored on an eight-yard run in the third quarter to give the Colonels a 7–0 lead.

In the fourth quarter, Nathan ran 15 yards but fumbled at the goal line. Woodlawn center Howard Caserbe fell on the ball in the end zone for a touchdown, which helped the Colonels walk away with a 14–0 victory. It was a good break. Nathan finished with 87 yards on 19 carries—earning every yard along the way—with one touchdown. Slowly but surely, the Colonels were figuring out that they were more than a one-man show. Woodlawn High's defense, led by McKinstry, linebacker Joe Abbruzzo, tackles Gil Wesley and James Morris, and end Howard Ross threw an impressive shutout against the Red Raiders.

Slowly but surely, the Colonels were figuring out
that they were more than a one-man show.

The next week against Vestavia Hills, Nathan showed he could still play defense, too. The Rebels drove deep into Woodlawn territory on their opening possession, but Nathan stepped in front of a pass and returned it 98 yards for a touchdown, which gave the Colonels a 6–0 lead. Both teams were plagued by turnovers throughout the contest, and Colonels tackle James Morris made two big fumble recoveries in the second half. After the second one, Rogers ran for a one-yard touchdown and Nathan ran for a two-point conversion to give the Colonels a 14–0 lead. Vestavia

Hills scored in the fourth quarter but couldn't get any closer in Woodlawn High's 14–8 win. Nathan finished with 148 rushing yards on 23 carries.

It took a similar yeoman's effort in a 20–9 victory over Erwin High School on October 3, as Nathan ran for 169 yards with one touchdown. When Huffman High's defense paid too much attention to Nathan the next week, Ragland took advantage with his passing. After the Colonels fell behind 7–0, Ragland threw a 42-yard touchdown pass to Jimmy Davis in the first quarter and then a 65-yard touchdown to him in third to give Woodlawn High a 19–7 lead. Nathan ran for 114 yards on 21 attempts in a 25–7 win.

The scary part: Rutledge and the rest of the first-team offense were barely breaking a sweat and sitting out the second half of most games.

After a 6–0 start, the Colonels were starting to feel pretty good. They hadn't yet hit their stride on offense, but Nathan was slowly getting healthy and their defense was playing as well as anybody in the city. Gerelds didn't have to worry about his team getting overconfident. Banks High School, which was ranked No. 1 in the state in Class 4A, was absolutely demolishing its opponents. The Jets won their first three games of the season against Carver High, Hayes High, and Ramsay High by a combined score of 174–0. Against Carver, the Jets intercepted five passes and led 27–0 at the end of the first quarter, 34–0 at the half, and 55–0 at the end of the third in a 62–0 victory. The scary part: Rutledge and the rest of the first-team offense were barely breaking a sweat and sitting out the second half of most games.

When the Jets defeated Huffman 35–0 on October 25, they tied a city record by going 33 consecutive games without a loss. Banks hadn't been defeated since losing to Woodlawn in the 1971 finale. The Jets tied Berry High 14–14 in the last regular season game of 1972, but they'd beaten everyone else since losing to the Colonels three years earlier. Now, Banks seemed to be on a collision course with Woodlawn again. Excitement and anticipation were building toward their November 8 showdown at Legion Field.

First, the No. 6–ranked Colonels had to get past Ramsay High and Jones Valley High before they'd get a chance against the Jets. Against Ramsay, Nathan scored 44 points on seven touchdowns and a two-point conversion—in less than three quarters of action. He ran for 228 yards on 13 carries and returned a kickoff 87 yards for a touchdown. The performance earned him a spot in *Sports Illustrated* on November 4, 1974, as he was featured in the popular magazine's "Faces in the Crowd" section. The Colonels had a much more difficult time the next week, barely surviving a 14–13 victory over Jones Valley. The Brownies went ahead 13–7 in the third quarter, but Hendrix blocked the point-after kick. The play proved to be the difference. After Hendrix recovered a fumble, Nathan's 15-yard touchdown run and the point-after kick put the Colonels ahead for good 14–13.

A week after the Colonels squeaked past Jones Valley, the Jets had a much easier time against the Brownies in a 35–7 victory at Lawson Field on November 1. The Colonels had an extra week to prepare and rest, and after watching the Jets play against Jones Valley, Gerelds was certain his team would need it.

CHAPTER TEN

TONY VS. JEFF

As Woodlawn High School prepared to play Banks High School on November 8, 1974, the Colonels saw the Goodyear Blimp fly above their practice field near the Birmingham airport. There was such anticipation and excitement surrounding the game that the Colonels thought the blimp was there to broadcast it.

"It came over our practice field, and we were all thinking it was there for us," Woodlawn High defensive end Howard Ross said.

The Goodyear Blimp was actually in Birmingham for ABC TV's broadcast of the University of Alabama's game against Louisiana State University, which was going to take place at Legion Field the day after the Colonels and Jets played there. Alabama was college football's defending national champion, having finished 11–1 in '73, and was a perfect 8–0 going into the LSU game. But even the Crimson Tide might have taken a backseat to the Colonels and Jets in Birmingham that week.

"Friday Night Lights" had never taken on such importance in the state where football always seemed to matter most. The Jets were ranked No. 1 in the state; the Colonels were No. 4. Both teams were undefeated and featured a superstar: Woodlawn High's Tony Nathan and Banks High's Jeff Rutledge. The best running back in the state was playing against the best quarterback. They'd squared off in each of the past two seasons, with Rutledge and the Jets winning both times, and this would be the Colonels' final opportunity to even the score with a victory in Nathan's senior season.

"It was being billed as the biggest game in the state—ever," Nathan said. "As far as I was concerned, it was just another game we were playing against a team I really wanted to beat. It was the team standing in our way."

Woodlawn defensive coordinator Jerry Stearns remembered making quite a few trips to the Birmingham Board of Education to get tickets to sell for the game. It seemed every time Woodlawn received a stack of tickets, its students gobbled them up during advance sales in the cafeteria. Banks High School coach Shorty White warned city school officials to expect a bigger crowd than usual. He called the manager of Legion Field and told him to treat their game like he would a college contest.

"I called him and told him if we were undefeated and Woodlawn High was undefeated, we were going to have the biggest crowd they'd ever had for a high school game," White said. "He told me they'd never had a high school game they couldn't handle."

It was obvious it wouldn't be a typical high school football game. The two competing Birmingham newspapers—*Birmingham News* and *Birmingham Post-Herald*—treated the buildup like they would a big college game or even a professional contest. The newspapers previewed the game throughout the week. The headline of the *News'* sports section on the day of the game read "SHOWDOWN: Banks and Woodlawn Put It All on the Line Tonight."

The Colonels knew what was at stake: if they didn't defeat the Jets, they wouldn't go to the state playoffs for the third season in a row. In a lot of ways, it was like the annual Iron Bowl between Alabama and Auburn deciding the Southeastern Conference's West Division title, with the winner advancing to the SEC championship game and the loser staying home.

The game seemed larger than life. By the time the Banks game arrived, Gerelds was almost relieved. He usually zoned out during game weeks by doodling constantly on a yellow legal pad, always looking for a new play or way to attack an opponent. But he had a different demeanor the week of the Banks High game and almost seemed more relaxed. The Colonels had survived the previous two months without a loss, and it was as if their entire existence that season depended on reaching the Banks High game with an unblemished record.

"When I think back on that week, I almost feel like he wasn't as tense that week as the weeks going up to it," said Debbie Gerelds. "There were so many things we had to go through and so many obstacles we had to get past."

The Jets also had much on the line. They'd now played 34 games in a row without losing; their last defeat had come at the hands of the Colonels, who beat them 21–18 at the end of the '71 regular season. Woodlawn had won 11 games in a row and hadn't lost since falling to Banks during the '73 season. Coach White, who guided the Jets to state championships in the previous two seasons, would also be going for his 100th victory at Banks High School. He wanted nothing more than to reach the milestone against the Colonels, the Jets' longtime rivals.

"We're just preparing to play a football game, not to play Banks," Gerelds told *The Birmingham News*. "They do too many things well. If we're not good enough to beat them, we sure can't trick them. We just have to play our game, not Banks' game."

The Jets were a much more experienced team. Of the fourteen Banks High players who were offensive starters, only Frank Gunnels and Jack Robertson were juniors. The rest were seniors, including Rutledge and running backs Jerry Murphree, Milton Miles, and Joe Wahl. Conversely, the Colonels were a relatively young team. During the '74 season, Gerelds used eight players who were playing on the varsity team for the first time, including running backs Billy Johnson and Dennis Rogers, who lined up in the backfield with Nathan. But Gerelds knew inexperience couldn't be an excuse against the Jets.

"They've given us outstanding effort, and they've improved a lot during the year," Gerelds told the *News*. "We had a good season and so has Banks. It all depends on this game as far as the state playoff is concerned. It's unfortunate we have to beat the No. 1 team in the nation to get there. I feel that on a given night we can beat anybody."

Of course, the spotlight was going be on Nathan and Rutledge. In early October, Rutledge and Nathan were among thirty high school players from around the country who were named the best college prospects in America by *Family Weekly* magazine. In an era before online recruiting services and cable TV (and strict NCAA recruiting rules), a panel of coaches from Alabama, Maryland, Michigan, Notre Dame, Oklahoma, Southern California, and Texas selected the team. Billy Sims, a running back from Hooks, Texas, who would win the Heisman Trophy as college football's best player in 1978, was also on the team. One of the panel's voters said of Nathan, "He's just a big kid with great speed. Everybody wants him."

Nathan and Rutledge more than lived up to their lofty reputations during their senior seasons. Nathan was being courted heavily by the University of Alabama, Auburn University, and the University of Tennessee, among dozens of other colleges. The Crimson Tide also badly wanted Rutledge, whose older brother Gary was already playing quarterback for them. But the younger Rutledge wondered if he wouldn't be better suited to play at LSU, which ran the veer offense, the same system the Jets used. LSU assistant coach Jerry Stovall attended every Banks High game in 1974 and was trying to convince Rutledge that he would have more opportunities to throw the ball in the Tigers' offense than in Alabama's wishbone system.

"He's just a big kid with great speed. Everybody wants him."

On the night before the game, players from both schools gathered at a Fellowship of Christian Athletes meeting at a Birmingham church. The teams sat on opposite sides of the church, but many of the players mingled and shook hands before the meeting.

"I remember staring at Jeff Rutledge and thinking, 'I wish there was something I could find that I don't like about him,'" Woodlawn offensive lineman Reginald Greene said. "I had to get motivated to play the game, but he was such a nice guy."

It was rare for opposing teams to attend the same event the night before they played a game. But the evangelist Wales Goebel and both teams' chaplains wanted the players together to reinforce what they'd been telling them during the past two seasons—that they were playing for the glory of God, and the spotlight on the next night's game was another opportunity for them to share the message.

These kids were about to play the biggest game of their lives; but on that night, it wasn't about state championships, about winning or losing, and it definitely was not about how many black versus white players were on each team. That night, it was about coming together with a common faith and worshipping God.

"It was amazing to see all those kids together," Stearns said. "When it was over, we went our separate ways. The next night, we made history together."

"When it was over, we went our separate ways.
The next night, we made history together."

As the Woodlawn High players and coaches made their way to Legion Field on Friday afternoon, they realized the game was going to be much different from the ones they'd played before. Their bus had a police escort to the field for the first time. As the Woodlawn caravan made its way down 8th Avenue North, there was already a long line of cars and trucks trying to make their way to the stadium—about three hours before kickoff. Once they reached the stadium, there was a crowd of children at the entrance asking for players' autographs.

Before leaving his house that morning, Gerelds warned his wife about the traffic, and she was determined to have her customary seat at the fifty-yard line. But after Debbie Gerelds, the other coaches' wives, and their children sat in the traffic jam on

Graymont Avenue for more than an hour, they were stunned to find thousands of people waiting outside Gate 7 at the south side of Legion Field. The fans, many of whom had converged on Birmingham from across the state and the South, were trying to get into the stadium.

"The kids were going crazy," Debbie Gerelds said. "We'd never missed a kickoff."

Legion Field's staff had not heeded Coach White's warning and wasn't prepared for the onslaught of people. Walter Garrett, who was the stadium manager at Legion Field for thirty-eight years, later told *The Birmingham News* that only Gates 7A and 7B were opened, which was customary for high school games.

"Each gate had four openings in it for four lines of people," Garrett said. "But it still obviously wasn't enough."

Many of the ticket holders wouldn't reach their seats until the second quarter because of the mob of people.

Somehow, while trying to keep up with her hyperactive son and young daughters, Debbie Gerelds made it through the swarming crowds to their seats. As always, she sat next to Louise Nathan. They'd become close friends over the past two years; Louise even sewed clothes for the Gereldses' children. Louise was probably the only fan in the stadium that might have been as loud as Debbie, which was probably why they enjoyed sitting next to each other.

Once everyone was finally in their seats, Legion Field officials estimated the crowd to be 42,000, which was by far the largest to ever watch a high school football game in Alabama. The previous attendance record for a high school game was 32,159 when Woodlawn High played Phillips High in the 1959 Crippled Children's Classic at Legion Field. Only two days earlier, a crowd of 22,963 fans watched the Birmingham Americans of the World Football League defeat the Philadelphia Bell 26–23. Nearly twice as many fans showed up to watch two high school teams play. Birmingham police estimated that another twenty thousand fans saw the crowds outside the stadium, turned around, and headed home.

Officials estimated the crowd to be 42,000,
which was by far the largest to ever watch a
high school football game in Alabama.

"It was shocking to see that many people at a game," Nathan said. "I saw crowds like that on TV, but not at a high school game. It was a little bit of a distraction seeing that many people. It was one of the few times that you really noticed how many people were there to watch a high school game."

During pregame warm-ups, Stearns glanced over at Woodlawn assistant coach Mike Logan, who was looking up at the crowd, with his jaw practically lying on the grass. Logan, who had spent the previous season at rural Locust Fork High School in Locust Fork, Alabama, had never seen a crowd so big for a high school game.

"What's wrong, Mike? They didn't have crowds like this at Locust Fork?" Stearns asked him.

College coaches flocked to Legion Field to see the game. Alabama coach Bear Bryant, Auburn coach Ralph "Shug" Jordan, LSU coach Charlie McClendon, and three other head coaches from Southeastern Conference teams watched the game from the press box, along with dozens of assistants from other colleges around the country. Celebrities such as ABC TV announcer Keith Jackson and novelist James Michener attended a dinner party with Birmingham VIPs on the first deck of the press box before the game.

Eventually, additional police officers were summoned to keep order at the gates, as students and other fans started climbing fences to get into the stadium. No one wanted to miss kickoff. Howard Ross's mother lost her purse as the crowd pushed her through the gates. It was so crowded that Legion Field officials twice delayed the game—for a total of thirty minutes—so fans could get through the gates and into their seats.

"I was mad because we were ready to play," Woodlawn quarterback Denny Ragland said. "When we came out, it was amazing. The entire lower level of the stadium was full, except for maybe a couple of sections in the end zones. It was really a sight to see."

It was like watching a heavyweight fight,
with both boxers dancing and feeling out his
opponent before making an assault.

Finally, after the long delays, Goebel delivered the pregame invocation and then fans heard the familiar voice of Simpson Pepper, the longtime public address announcer, who welcomed the fans to Legion Field. At the start, the players from both sides appeared nervous and overwhelmed. Both teams struggled to move the ball on offense, and it seemed neither team was willing to take a chance that might result in a big mistake. It was like watching a heavyweight fight, with both boxers dancing and feeling out his opponent before making an assault.

One thing was clear: Woodlawn High's defense wasn't going to sit back and let Rutledge pick it apart. He'd sat out the Jets' previous game—a 35–7 victory over Jones Valley High—to rest his badly bruised thigh. Stearns knew Rutledge wasn't completely healthy, so he planned to blitz on defense early and often, which is something the Colonels rarely did. Rutledge was sacked seven times in the game, with Rocha McKinstry, Gil Wesley, and Howard Ross doing much of the damage. The high-octane Jets were held without a first down in the first quarter.

Late in the second quarter, though, Rutledge ran a veer play, and Jerry Murphree broke loose for a 21-yard touchdown. The Jets missed the extra point kick, leaving them with a 6–0 lead. After the Colonels turned the ball over, Banks needed only two plays to find the end zone again. Rutledge threw a 22-yard pass to Jerry McDonald and then a 32-yard touchdown to Bob Grefseng, a seldom-used tight end. It was the only touchdown catch of Grefseng's high school career and came on a busted play. Rutledge was pressured on what was supposed to be a quick pass, but he somehow found Grefseng open down the field. The Jets failed to convert a two-point play and had a 12–0 lead at the half.

Banks's plan for slowing down Woodlawn's offense was simple and effective: the Jets had to contain Nathan and not let him get outside the tackles. If Nathan was able to get into the open field, the Jets knew they'd have a hard time catching him. Greg Muse, a smallish linebacker, who had moved to Birmingham from Texas before the 1974 season, was charged with stalking Nathan on nearly every play. Unfortunately for the Colonels, Muse did his job very well for most of the game.

At the start of the second half, the Jets ate up more than six minutes off the clock while driving to Woodlawn's 14-yard line.

However, Banks picked up a 15-yard penalty and then Rutledge was sacked for a 13-yard loss, backing it out of scoring position. The Colonels were forced to punt on their ensuing possession, and then Rutledge needed only four plays to drive 51 yards for another touchdown. He threw a 23-yard pass to Wahl, ran for four yards, and then threw a six-yard pass to McDonald. Murphree scored his second touchdown on a 16-yard run, and the Jets had an 18–0 lead after another two-point conversion failed.

Finally, the Colonels scored early in the fourth quarter, when Nathan broke a couple of tackles and bounced outside for a 13-yard touchdown on fourth-and-one. Woodlawn High kicked the point-after to make it 18–7, but it was too little too late. Banks High won the game 18–7, beating the Colonels for the fourth straight season. The Jets extended their streak to 35 consecutive games without a loss, and assured themselves of making the state playoffs.

"Even though I've played on two state champion teams, I think this game meant more than any other," Murphree told *The Birmingham News*.

Nathan ran 31 times for 112 yards with one touchdown, but the Jets did an admirable job of bottling him up for most of the night. Making matters worse, the Colonels completed only one pass in the game. After the long delays to start the game, Woodlawn's offense never got on track.

"We didn't put on the offensive show we should have," Gerelds told the *News*. "We were ready to go at 7:20. The game delay might have had an effect on the team. We got off to a slow tempo. Banks just gutted up and played a whale of a game against us. They were outstanding all over the field."

Despite facing so much pressure from Woodlawn High's defense, Rutledge was nearly perfect throwing the ball, completing nine of 10 passes for 185 yards with one touchdown. Murphree ran 14 times for 99 yards with two touchdowns. But the story of the game was Banks High's defense, which never let the Colonels get going on offense.

"This wasn't Rutledge versus Nathan but Banks versus Woodlawn," Banks High tackle Fred Knighton said. "I would have to say that Woodlawn is the second best team in the state."

"This wasn't Rutledge versus Nathan
but Banks versus Woodlawn."

The victory took a physical toll on the Jets, who lost three defensive starters to injuries in the game. Their unbeaten streak ended the next week when Rutledge broke his ankle in a 34–27 loss to West End High. Without Rutledge, the Jets lost to eventual Class 4A state champion Homewood High Patriots 12–0 in the second round of the playoffs (they had a bye in the first round).

It wasn't the ending either the Colonels or Jets envisioned. Woodlawn rebounded to defeat Carver High School 12–0 at Lawson Field the next week, which gave them a 9–1 record. Still, the season seemed incomplete without defeating the Jets. The Colonels would never get to see Nathan and his fellow seniors in the state playoffs.

"It was very disappointing," Howard Ross said. "You have to move on and live with it. It's one of those things. We fought as hard as we could, but we just came up short."

Gerelds took the loss particularly hard. He knew his team deserved to be in the playoffs, but it could never get past the Jets.

"I had a hard time accepting the loss to Banks," Gerelds wrote shortly before his death. "I cared so much for those great kids. I was ashamed I couldn't give them a way to win. I have always felt that I was cheating kids on the field or in the classroom if I did not give them all I had each day. It takes an enormous amount of energy and enthusiasm to keep performing this way."

Gerelds second-guessed himself many times over the next few months, wondering what else he could have done to help his team win.

"I think it was one of the biggest disappointments in Tandy's coaching life," Debbie Gerelds said. "I think he felt that those kids deserved so much to go to the state playoffs. He knew they worked as hard as they could possibly have worked. He may have been hearing the voice in his head in the final seconds, asking himself what he could have done."

It was a game many of the players would remember for the rest of their lives—the night Woodlawn High School played Banks High School in front of 42,000 fans at Legion Field.

"Years later, it's amazing how many people you run into who say they were at that game," Colonels defensive back Steve Martin said. "If you believe everybody, there must have been seventy-five thousand people there."

CHAPTER ELEVEN

THE VOICE

Debbie Gerelds remembers waking up many nights and not finding her husband in bed. She would often find him in the kitchen, watching film of plays over and over again. When Tandy Gerelds was coaching, he rarely left his work at the office; the wheels in his head were always turning, as he searched for any advantage to help his team win.

"If they lose the ball game, I'm fine with that," Tandy often told his wife. "If I cause them to lose the game, I can't live with that."

The fear of failure is the reason Debbie often found Tandy in the kitchen with a projector late at night.

"I really think he believed with all of his heart that if the kids won, it's because they did what they were coached to do," Debbie said. "But if they ever lost a game, it's because he didn't do his job good enough. It was never the players' fault."

Perhaps no defeat disappointed Gerelds as much as Woodlawn High School's 18–7 loss to Banks High during the '74 season. It was a bitter defeat that haunted him for the rest of his coaching career. Gerelds knew the Colonels had squandered a golden opportunity to compete for a state championship—if they'd only qualified for the playoffs. He wanted so much more for star tailback Tony Nathan and for his fellow seniors—who'd never beaten the Jets or made the playoffs during their three seasons on Woodlawn's varsity team. Gerelds believed that those players, who helped save his program through their unselfishness and commitment to God and each other, deserved a better ending to their high school careers.

Over the next several months, he often wondered what he could have done differently.

"I always felt that anything that went wrong on the football field was a direct reflection on me," Gerelds wrote before his death. "Once again, I had to deal with stress and pressure. I know now that I put too much pressure on myself."

"I always felt that anything that went wrong on the football field was a direct reflection on me," Gerelds wrote.

Many of Woodlawn High's best players moved on after the 1974 season, including Nathan, who had carried so much of the load on offense during the previous two seasons. Defensive lineman Brad Hendrix, offensive lineman Reginald Greene, and linebacker Rocha McKinstry had also graduated.

Replacing Nathan and the other departed starters in '75 wouldn't be easy. Making matters worse, the Colonels lost fullback Dennis Rogers to a knee injury during spring practice, which would sideline him for the start of the season. Frank Craddock replaced Denny Ragland as the team's starting quarterback, and returning wingback Billy Johnson, fullback Frank D'Amico, and tailback Derrick May joined him in the backfield. At five-foot-nine and 170 pounds, May was a much different runner than Nathan. With tackle Gil Wesley, linebacker Joe Abbruzzo, and defensive back Roger Langston coming back, the Colonels would have to lean mightily on their defense.

"Naturally, we've changed a lot around," Gerelds told *The Birmingham News* before the 1975 season. "There are things we did with Tony that we just can't do anymore. We'll have to play more straight football, and we'll have to block. Of course, we've had some pretty good blocking for the past couple of years, but we're going to have to do some more. We were playing football at Woodlawn long before Tony came. That's not to say we're not going to miss him, but now we'll just have to do without him."

The Colonels ended up adjusting pretty well. Woodlawn High started the 1975 season by winning its first six games, shutting out three opponents along the way, before losing to Berry High 12–3 on October 17. The Colonels bounced back to win their next two games, including a 12–0 victory over Banks High at Legion Field on November 7. Woodlawn's defense intercepted three passes and recovered two fumbles, allowing the Colonels to finally get over the hump with their first victory against the Jets since 1971. But Gerelds wasn't on the sideline for the game: he had literally worried himself sick while preparing for the game. The Colonels dedicated the contest to their bedridden coach, and longtime defensive coordinator Jerry Stearns directed the squad during the game.

Woodlawn finished the regular season with an 8–1 record and won the Class 4A Region 9 championship. With Gerelds back on the sideline a week later, the Colonels lost to Tuscaloosa County High School 19–0 in the first round of the Class 4A state playoffs. It was the last game Gerelds would coach at Woodlawn High.

In January 1976, Gerelds resigned as head coach at Wood-lawn High School after posting a 36–14 record in five seasons. He spent eleven seasons as a teacher, assistant, and head coach at his alma mater, and leaving the sideline and classroom wasn't an easy decision. But the pressure to win consistently was becoming too much of a burden. Gerelds had become his own worst critic. He was once again consumed by winning—and even more so by the fear of losing. His health declined throughout the 1975 season—so much so that Debbie feared he might suffer a nervous breakdown.

"He used to tell me that people do things for a living, but nobody tells the dentist how to fill a tooth, nobody tells a car salesman how to sell a car, and nobody tells a plumber how to fix a pipe," Debbie said. "But everybody thinks they're a coach. He knew his work was on a football field in front of thousands of people watching, and they're all judging his work."

Even though Gerelds had become one of the most successful high school coaches in Birmingham, he was never satisfied with anything but perfection. Before his death, Gerelds described the pressure he put on himself while coaching and explained why he decided to step away from the sideline in 1976:

> It's like the walk down the hall to the electric chair or gas chamber like you see on TV or in the movies. The only difference is you know you are going to live to do it again. You're crazy, maybe so. That will be the first thing people might think about me. The only people who can sympathize with me are other coaches. Why is this fear there and how do you deal with it?
>
> First, most coaches want to keep a macho image, so they never let on that it will affect them. No one wants to admit that they

are scared, so they hide it in various ways. Some act nonchalantly, others put on a game face, some hide it in flamboyant, fired-up speeches, and some even direct the problem toward their players so it will take some of their fear away. But the fear is there because you don't want to get beat. It is normal. What is not normal is to get beat or embarrassed in front of your friends, neighbors, and anyone else who might have attended the game. The fear of getting beat, which is embarrassing to anyone, is a force that drives anyone who competes. Sometimes it seems to engulf you and you feel like it is a life-or-death struggle. That's when you start that walk down the hall to the execution. It's also when you need to stop and say, "This is a game played by kids for fun. How can I make it fun for them?"

"There has always been a voice inside me telling me I can't fail. It tells me I have to win and that if I don't, I'm nothing."

There has always been a voice inside me telling me I can't fail. It tells me I have to win and that if I don't, I'm nothing and at the bottom of the barrel. Ever since I can remember, the voice has always been there. As a twelve-year-old, I can remember being heartbroken because I did not perform up to high standards. I can also remember accomplishments never being quite good enough for me. I have always wanted to be the very best at what I do. I just never thought that was possible until now.

I feel like God has let me be the best I can be. It is a blessing that very few people get to have. I just praise God because without Him I would still be trying for the impossible. The voice is gone now. Praise God, and I can finally rest.

Gerelds turned the Woodlawn program over to defensive co-ordinator Jerry Stearns, his close friend, who would coach the Colonels for the next twenty-three seasons and then Kingwood Christian School in Alabaster, Alabama, for ten more. After leaving Woodlawn High School, Gerelds took a job working with his father, Tommy Gerelds, who owned an insurance business in the community. More than anything else, Gerelds wanted to spend more time with his wife and three children. At the time he retired from coaching, daughter Jessica was ten years old, son Todd was eight, and his younger daughter, Jill, was four. Gerelds felt his life was out of balance. After much prayer and reflection, he decided it was time to help his wife raise their children:

> I married Debbie when she was eighteen years old and very immature. We had our first child, Jessica, when she was twenty. I can never remember her complaining about raising the baby. I was never at home and when I was, I wasn't much help. I lived and breathed football and coaching, and didn't take time to be a good husband and father. Debbie complained about me loving my job more than her or Jessica, and she was probably right. For some reason, she stayed with me and supported me in anything I did.
>
> Two years after Jessica was born, my son, Todd, came into the world. Debbie would bundle him up and drag Jessica to all the football games. She always accepted the responsibility of raising our kids and never complained about them—only me. I hope I added a little to the raising of the kids from a stability standpoint, but Debbie was the key to keeping our family together.

Gerelds spent the next eight years working at his father's insurance agency on 1st Avenue in Birmingham. Eventually, he bought the agency from his father and seemed ready to spend the rest of his career running the business. Gerelds was appointed to the board of directors of Alabama Independent Insurance Agents and became a trusted businessman in the city. But in the back of Gerelds's mind, he knew his true calling was coaching and teaching young people. In 1984, Gerelds enrolled at the University of Alabama at Birmingham and renewed his state teaching certificate. He applied for several head coaching jobs around the state, but didn't receive much immediate response. Gerelds began to worry that he'd spent too much time away from the game.

Bob Haggard, who was the principal at Deshler High School in Tuscumbia, Alabama, was a former football coach in Birmingham and knew Gerelds's reputation. Two Deshler High assistants interviewed for the vacancy, but Haggard and superintendent Bob Clemmons decided to hire Gerelds. His hiring wasn't well received in Tuscumbia. Many residents wondered why they chose a coach who hadn't been on the sideline in nine seasons. For the first time in his career, Gerelds felt unwanted:

The administration took some abuse for hiring me. The administration, however, did not take the abuse that I did. I didn't know how to handle it. This was something new. I had always been well liked, respected, and wanted. People did not like me for the simple reason that I got a job that they wanted someone else to have.

I had come to Tuscumbia with a vision of building a good athletic program, and at the same time raising my family in a wholesome environment. I was hoping to fit into the small town as the coach. This turned out to be only a vision, not reality. I tried to make friends and be nice to people. I thought that was the answer.

I soon found out what most people already knew: you can't please everyone and everyone is not going to like you.

At Deshler High School, Gerelds inherited a football program with a $45,000 deficit. Its football facilities were in disrepair, and there wasn't any money to improve them because of declining attendance. Deshler hadn't produced a winning season since 1980 and was coming off a 3–7 campaign in 1983.

Prior to the 1984 season, Gerelds decided to re-create the "Woodlawn Camp" experience for his new team. The Tigers loaded onto buses and headed to rural Cullman, Alabama, to a monastery called Saint Bernard Abbey. This time, Gerelds actually invited Wales Goebel and other Christian speakers to camp. Several players came to Christ during that camp, including Gerelds's son, Todd. The preseason camp became a tradition at Deshler High that God used in the lives of the players and that served to bond the teams in a unique way.

Much like at Woodlawn High School, Gerelds needed all the help he could find at the start of his tenure. The Tigers played so poorly in 1984 that Gerelds offered to resign midway through the season.

"I asked God to give me the wisdom to do things right and started trying to build some enthusiasm for the program," Gerelds told the Florence, Alabama, *Times Daily* in 1994. "But my ways were different from what had been done in the past. I decided no one would outwork my staff. That wasn't what the coaches and players were looking for. I made some decisions, but some people did not like them and voiced their opinion. Before we even played a game, some people asked me to leave."

Before long, however, many Tuscumbia residents wanted Gerelds to coach at Deshler High School forever. The Tigers won three of their final four games during his first season in 1984, earning the first of eleven consecutive appearances in the state playoffs. In '87, Deshler went 11–2, losing its season opener and then in the fourth round of the state playoffs. In 1990, the Tigers went a perfect 15–0 and won the Class 4A state championship. They set a state scoring record with 600 points. The next season, Deshler High won its first 13 games before losing to T. R. Miller High School 46–6 in the state championship game, which ended the school's 28-game winning streak.

Under Gerelds's direction, the Tigers went 101–36 from 1984 to 1994, with 19 of those defeats coming against opponents in higher classifications. As athletics director, Gerelds helped Deshler High construct a new field house and press box at Howard Chappell Stadium, as well as improve the playing field and sprinkler system. He retired as the Tigers' coach after the 1994 season. In 2003, Tuscumbia honored Gerelds by renaming the area at Dickson Street and Woodmont Drive as Tandy Gerelds Memorial Drive.

"I accomplished what they asked me to do in 1984," Gerelds told the Florence *Times Daily*. "We have great facilities, the coaching staff is unified, we're out of the red. We gave the city something to be proud of. Mainly, we gave some kids an opportunity to be something special. They took the opportunity and made something of themselves."

After spending the 1995–96 school year as Deshler High's golf coach, Gerelds retired a second time and was out of work the next two years. In 1998, he was named the principal at Shoals Christian School in Florence, Alabama. Gerelds started the school's football program the next year and served as the Flames' head coach until he stepped down in 2001. In 2004, Shoals Christian School renamed its stadium Flame Field in honor and memory of Tandy Gerelds and Dr. Bill Trapp. Trapp, one of Gerelds's close friends and a cofounder of the school, died of Lou Gehrig's disease in 2000.

"He always knew when it was time for him to leave a place," Debbie said of her husband. "He would tell me, 'The Lord has told me it's time to move on.'"

When Gerelds left Shoals Christian School in 2001, Debbie thought he was retiring from coaching and teaching for good. But then an assistant principal from Belmont High School in Belmont, Mississippi, asked Gerelds if he would be interested in the head coaching vacancy there. Belmont was about forty-four miles from Gerelds's home in Tuscumbia, so it would be a two-hour round-trip commute. Gerelds took the Belmont coaching job, along with serving as director of the county's alternative school for students with disciplinary problems or other behavioral issues.

The residents of Belmont were excited to have such an accomplished coach at their school and immediately accepted him.

"The Lord puts you in the place where you need to be," Debbie said. "It was such a sweet, loving community. Tandy told me I would love it. He said it was like being in the 1960s. It was such a slower pace. They were so excited about getting a coach who had won a state championship in Alabama. They thought he was Bear Bryant."

As Gerelds had done at his previous stops, he immediately started to try to build Belmont High into a winner. In the summer of 2002, Gerelds spent nearly every day working on a practice field, so the Cardinals wouldn't tear up the playing surface at their stadium. As Gerelds worked in the stifling Mississippi heat, he became more and more fatigued. After he nearly ran over his golf bag with his cart following a round with friends, and then couldn't write one of his player's names on a whiteboard during a staff meeting, he knew something was wrong. An MRI revealed that he had stage 4 lung cancer.

An MRI revealed that Gerelds had stage 4 lung cancer.

"The town was devastated," Debbie said. "His players and coaches were devastated."

Even with a grim prognosis, Gerelds vowed to finish what he started at Belmont High. Despite receiving daily radiation treatments and chemotherapy once a week, Gerelds never missed a practice or game during the 2002 season. Since doctors didn't want him driving, Debbie drove her husband to Belmont High after his 7 a.m. radiation treatments. The nurses at the hospital where she worked agreed to adjust their shifts so she could do it. During Gerelds's treatment, he went to a healing service with his sister. The pastor asked him, "Would you ask for more time?"

"I think we all have a designated amount of time," Gerelds told him.

"You wouldn't want any more time?" the pastor asked.

"Well, I guess I'd want three more months because I told those kids I'd get them through the season," Gerelds said.

Before the Cardinals played their first game in 2002, the players shaved their heads to honor their coach, who had lost his hair as a side effect of his cancer treatment. Belmont finished 5–5 and advanced to the state playoffs.

"There was no other place the Lord could have had us to meet so many special people," Debbie said. "It was a blessing. There was a reason for us to be there."

Tandy Gerelds died on January 10, 2003, after a brief but valiant battle against cancer. His obituary described him as many things: "a loving husband, a well-respected and well-beloved father, a dedicated coach, a servant-hearted deacon, and a compassionate and caring friend."

For the men who played for Gerelds, he was so much more than a coach. For some of his players, Gerelds was the closest thing to a father they'd ever had.

CHAPTER TWELVE

CHAMPIONS

On New Year's Day 1979, Tandy Gerelds sat in the living room of his home in Birmingham, Alabama, preparing to watch the University of Alabama play Penn State University in the Sugar Bowl. In what would become one of the most epic games in college football history, two of the sport's most storied programs—and two men who would become its most exalted coaches—were about to square off in the Louisiana Superdome in New Orleans.

Legendary Alabama coach Bear Bryant was attempting to win his fifth national championship, after narrowly missing one the previous season, when the Crimson Tide finished 11–1 and defeated Ohio State 35–6 in the Sugar Bowl. Penn State coach Joe Paterno, after several near misses of his own, was hoping to guide the undefeated Nittany Lions to their first national championship.

While the game would be watched in living rooms and watering holes across the country, Gerelds had a personal interest in the contest. Tony Nathan, his former star tailback at Woodlawn High School, was preparing to play in his final game at Alabama. So was Crimson Tide quarterback Jeff Rutledge, the former Banks High School star who had spoiled the Colonels' memorable seasons in 1973 and 1974. Ironically, Shorty White, who guided the Jets to three state titles, was Nathan's running backs coach at Alabama. White had left Banks High in 1975 and would be a member of Bryant's staff until 1980.

Unlike at Woodlawn High School, Nathan didn't have to break color barriers to become a star player for the Crimson Tide. Bryant opened the door for desegregating Alabama's football team by scheduling a game against the University of Southern California in the 1970 season opener. Alabama won three national championships under Bryant during the 1960s but slipped to 8–3 in 1968 and then 6–5 in 1969. The Crimson Tide still had a lily-white roster, as other schools around the country integrated their teams. For years, Bryant defended accusations of racism by saying the state's social climate didn't allow him to recruit African American players. But as Bryant's program slipped into mediocrity, he knew changes had to be made.

On September 12, 1970, USC embarrassed the Crimson Tide 42–21 at Legion Field in Birmingham. Sam Cunningham, an African American player, ran for 135 yards with two touchdowns—needing only 12 carries to do it against Alabama's all-white defense. Black players scored each of the Trojans' touchdowns, including one by Birmingham-born Clarence Davis. The Trojans piled up 559 yards of offense, nearly 300 more than the Crimson Tide, and the unforgettable defeat was enough to convince Alabama fans that Bryant would have to recruit African American players if his teams were going to continue to compete for national championships. Alabama assistant Jerry Claiborne famously said of the USC loss, "Sam Cunningham did more to integrate Alabama in sixty minutes that night than Martin Luther King had accomplished in twenty years."

While the loss to USC had a profound impact on the future of Alabama's program, Bryant had actually broken the color barrier prior to the game. Before the 1970 season, he recruited wide receiver Wilbur Jackson of Ozark, Alabama, who agreed to become the first African American football player to accept a scholarship from the Crimson Tide. Jackson didn't play during the 1970 season because freshmen were ineligible to play under NCAA rules at the time. In 1971, John Mitchell transferred from Eastern Arizona College and became the first black player to appear in a game for the Crimson Tide. Bryant's decision to integrate Alabama's roster paid immediate dividends. The Crimson Tide won a national championship in 1973 (they were ranked No. 1 by United Press International even after losing to Notre Dame 24–23 in the Sugar Bowl) and claimed an SEC title in every season but one from 1971 to 1977.

"Sam Cunningham did more to integrate Alabama
in sixty minutes that night than Martin Luther
King had accomplished in twenty years."

Pioneers such as Jackson, Mitchell, and the other African American players who soon followed them to Alabama made Nathan's college choice much easier. Nearly every major college program in the country was recruiting Nathan, but he narrowed his choices to Alabama, Auburn, and Tennessee during his senior year at Woodlawn High. Nathan still wanted to play basketball in college—he was an all-state guard for the Colonels—and, for a while, even considered not playing football at all. But Bryant turned up the heat on Nathan to get him to stay close to home. Bryant brought popular Alabama quarterback Joe Namath and star tailback Johnny Musso to Nathan's home to persuade him to play for Alabama. Bryant told Nathan that he needed to play for the Crimson Tide if he wanted to win championships.

Nathan's parents were impressed that the most famous man in Alabama was so interested in their son. Louise Nathan preferred Alabama because it was close to home, and, just as important, Bryant liked to have multiple running backs carrying the ball. She didn't want her son running the ball in college as much as he had in high school. Pops Nathan liked Bryant even more after he ate and complimented his signature raccoon dish during a recruiting visit to their home.

When it was time for high school seniors to choose their colleges in December 1974, Nathan still wasn't sure where he wanted to go. Alabama tried to send an assistant coach to his house on December 14, 1974, which was the start of the signing period for Southeastern Conference schools. But Nathan wanted to be alone with his family as he pondered what to do; he didn't want outside influences as he made the biggest decision of his life. It was also his eighteenth birthday. Initially, Nathan was so torn about what to do that he thought about delaying his decision until after basketball season. When Rutledge and twenty other players signed with the Crimson Tide, Nathan decided to wait.

But on December 19, Nathan decided to play for Alabama, choosing to stay close to home so he could attend the same college as his longtime girlfriend, Johnnie. He held a news conference at a restaurant near Woodlawn High School, and Bryant and Alabama basketball coach C. M. Newton attended the event. At the time, Nathan said he might want to play both sports in college as a freshman (the NCAA changed its rules to make fresh-men eligible for competition in 1972). Although Nathan briefly joined Alabama's basketball team during his freshman year, Bry-ant convinced Nathan to stay with football by promoting him to Alabama's varsity team on the second day of preseason workouts in 1975. By the time Nathan arrived at Alabama, the Crimson Tide's roster was nearly one-third black. Jackson and Calvin Cul-liver, another African American, led the Crimson Tide in rush-ing in 1973 and 1974, respectively. After Nathan signed with Alabama, he spent his first three seasons playing behind Johnny Davis, another black player. Nathan showed a lot of promise at Alabama, but he had to prove his abilities as a blocker—something he rarely did at Woodlawn High—to earn Bryant's confidence. He carried the ball only 20 times as a freshman, and then averaged 6.4 yards per carry with seven touchdowns as a sophomore. In Alabama's 38–7 rout of Auburn in the 1976 Iron Bowl at Legion Field in Birmingham, Nathan ran for 141 yards with two touchdowns. It was only the eighth time in the rivalry's history that a Crimson Tide player ran for more than 100 yards against the Tigers.

Nathan had to prove his abilities as a
blocker to earn Bryant's confidence.

"At Alabama, I had to block to play," Nathan said. "I knew that when I arrived there, but it wasn't an easy thing to accept. Still, it was good training for me, solid discipline. I learned one favor deserves another. I had to block for my fellow halfback so he would block for me—and that one hand watches what the other hand does. Unselfishness and fundamentals are what I learned most playing for Coach Bryant."

As a junior in 1977, Nathan led the Southeastern Conference with 6.2 yards per rushing attempt and scored 15 touchdowns, which was one shy of the school's single-season record. The Crimson Tide finished 11–1 in 1977, but Notre Dame was voted No. 1 in the final polls after defeating Texas 38–10 in the Cotton Bowl. After going 10–1 during the 1978 regular season, Alabama was on the verge of winning another national title if it could beat Penn State in Nathan's final college game. Once rivals and now college teammates, Nathan and Rutledge were one victory away from winning a championship together.

The 1979 Sugar Bowl was a defensive stalemate for most of the first half. Finally, with just over a minute left in the half, Nathan broke free for a long run. He gained 37 yards on two plays to take the Crimson Tide to Penn State's 30-yard line. Then Rutledge fired a 30-yard touchdown pass to Bruce Bolton, which gave Alabama a 7–0 lead at the half.

As Coach Gerelds watched the game from home, he reflected fondly on his early days with Nathan in the rivalry with Rutledge. Though he still sometimes heard that voice in his head reminding him of past imperfections, he took some pride in the role he had played in Nathan's development.

As the game continued, the Nittany Lions tied the score at 7–7 late in the third quarter. After Rutledge threw an interception, Penn State quarterback Chuck Fusina threw a 17-yard touchdown to Scott Fitzkee in the end zone. Then Alabama's Lou Ikner returned a punt 62 yards to the Nittany Lions' 11-yard line. Three plays later, running back Major Ogilvie ran for an eight-yard touchdown to put the Crimson Tide back in front 14–7.

Late in the fourth quarter, Penn State's Matt Millen forced a fumble on an option play, which the Nittany Lions recovered at Alabama's 19-yard line. Penn State drove to the eight, where it faced first-and-goal. The Nittany Lions would have four opportunities for a touchdown to tie the score. They gained two yards on first down, and then Fusina threw a pass to Fitzkee, who was hammered by Alabama's Don McNeal just as he reached the goal line. On third down, Alabama's defense stuffed fullback Matt Suhey for no gain, leaving Penn State one more chance to score.

On fourth down, Crimson Tide linebacker Barry Krause stopped tailback Matt Gunman for no gain. Alabama's defense held. Krause's play would be remembered as one of the biggest tackles in college football history, as the Crimson Tide held on for a 14–7 victory. Nathan ran 21 times for 127 yards, while Rutledge completed eight of 15 passes for 91 yards with one touchdown and two interceptions. The AP voted Alabama No. 1 in its final rankings, while UPI picked USC, which had defeated the Crimson Tide 24–14 at Legion Field during the regular season and beat Michigan 17–10 in the Rose Bowl.

Nathan ran 21 times for 127 yards, while Rutledge completed eight of 15 passes for 91 yards with one touchdown and two interceptions.

"We went out and earned what we got, and that's a great feeling," Nathan said. "It put the icing on the cake in the last year of my college career. Just to be a part of something on that stage was great. You don't know what tomorrow holds, and not everybody can say they've done that. That was our moment."

During his four seasons at Alabama, Nathan helped the Crimson Tide compile a 42–6 record from 1975 to 1978. He had his best college season as a senior, running 111 times for 770 yards with six touchdowns. He also caught 13 passes for 104 yards with one touchdown and had 401 yards on punt and kickoff returns. Nathan finished his college career with 3,362 all-purpose yards.

The Miami Dolphins selected Nathan in the third round (61st overall) of the 1979 NFL draft. In his first NFL season, he was mostly a kick returner and set a Dolphins rookie record with 1,603 all-purpose yards. Nathan played each of his nine NFL seasons with the Dolphins, helping them reach Super Bowl XVII in 1983 and Super Bowl XIX in 1985. In the 27–17 loss to the Washington Redskins in Super Bowl XVII on January 30, 1983, Nathan ran seven times for 26 yards. In the Dolphins' 38–16 loss to the San Francisco 49ers in Super Bowl XIX on January 20, 1985, he ran five times for 18 yards and caught 10 passes for 83 yards. His 10 receptions were the second most by a player in the Super Bowl at the time.

Nathan's 10 receptions during Super Bowl XIX were the second most by a player in the Super Bowl at the time.

Nathan's pro career is perhaps most remembered for his performance in the Dolphins' 41–38 loss in overtime to the San Diego Chargers in an AFC divisional playoff game on January

2, 1982, which became known as the "Epic in Miami." Nathan gained 162 total yards and scored twice against the Chargers, including a touchdown in which he caught a lateral from Duriel Harris near the goal line just before halftime.

Nathan finished his NFL career with 3,543 rushing yards, 3,592 receiving yards, and 32 total touchdowns. He retired from playing in 1988 and became an assistant under Dolphins coach Don Shula. In 1996, Nathan was hired as running backs coach of the Tampa Bay Buccaneers under Tony Dungy. He later worked as an assistant coach at Florida International University and with the NFL's Baltimore Ravens and the San Francisco 49ers.

In 1979, Nathan married his Woodlawn High sweetheart, the former Johnnie Wilson. They have three children. He now works as a bailiff for Miami-Dade County Court judge Edward Newman, his former Dolphins teammate. His parents still live in Birmingham.

Rutledge played 14 seasons in the NFL. Selected in the ninth round (246th overall) by the Los Angeles Rams in the 1979 NFL draft, Rutledge was mostly a backup quarterback in the pros and played on two Super Bowl–winning teams. He was a backup for the New York Giants when they defeated the Denver Broncos 39–20 in Super Bowl XXI on January 25, 1987, and with the Washington Redskins when they beat the Buffalo Bills 37–24 in Super Bowl XXVI on January 26, 1992. Rutledge was also a member of the St. Louis Rams when they lost to the Pittsburgh Steelers 31–19 in Super Bowl XIV on January 20, 1980.

After retiring from the NFL in 1993, Rutledge was hired as an assistant coach at Vanderbilt University in 1995. He was head coach at Montgomery Bell Academy in Nashville, Tennessee, winning state titles in 2002 and 2003. He later coached quarter-

backs for the NFL's Arizona Cardinals and the New York Senti-
nels of the United Football League, and was head coach at Pope
John Paul II High School in Hendersonville, Tennessee, and Valley Christian High School in Chandler, Arizona.

Rutledge married the former Laura Holmes, who watched
Banks High School defeat Woodlawn High from the stands at
Legion Field in 1974. She wasn't a student at either school, but
drove from Tuscaloosa to see the game. The next year, a Fellowship of Christian Athletes advisor suggested that Rutledge invite
Holmes to the Alabama team banquet following his freshman
season. They've been married for nearly four decades and have
three children.

Two other players from the 1974 Woodlawn High team
went on to play in the NFL. Defensive lineman Brad Hendrix,
who played at North Alabama with Woodlawn High teammates
Reginald Greene and Howard Ross, was in training camp with
the Dallas Cowboys during the 1979 season and the San Diego
Chargers from 1980 to 1982. Ross signed with the Oakland
Raiders as an undrafted free agent in 1979. Ross later returned
to Woodlawn High as an assistant coach and still teaches in Birmingham schools.

Many of the players from the 1973–74 Woodlawn High
teams built successful careers in other areas. They became ministers, bankers, educators, newsmen, and policemen. Quarterback Ronald Mumm, a starter on the 1973 team, joined the Air
Force ROTC program at Auburn University. He flew F-15 and
F-16 fighters for two decades and was an instructor at the United
States Air Force Fighter Weapons School. He was even the com-
manding officer of the famous Thunderbirds demonstration
team. Linebacker Jay Blackwood is a veterinarian in Florida, and

quarterback Denny Ragland built a successful career in banking. Hendrix became an investment banker and operates his own firm in Birmingham.

More than four decades ago, they played their unforgettable game against Banks High School at Legion Field. The Banks-Woodlawn rivalry lasted until 1988, when Banks High was converted into a middle school. Its high school students were fed into Woodlawn High until the Birmingham Board of Education closed the crumbling middle school in 2008. Even Legion Field, which was once known as the "Old Gray Lady" and the "Football Capital of the South," is a shell of what it once was. The University of Alabama no longer plays games there, and its only regular tenant, the University of Alabama-Birmingham, dropped its football program after the 2014 season (UAB announced in June 2015 that it planned to reinstate its program possibly as early as 2016). The stadium's upper deck was removed in 2004 because it wasn't structurally sound, and the neighborhood surrounding the stadium is one of the most dangerous urban areas in America.

Many former Woodlawn High players credit Gerelds for helping shape their lives, and they'll never forget when Wales Goebel invited them to ask Jesus Christ into their hearts.

Even though it was long ago, many of the former Woodlawn High players credit Gerelds for helping shape their lives, and they'll never forget the hot, sweltering night in 1973 when the evangelist Wales Goebel invited them to ask Jesus Christ into their hearts. The unforgettable night changed the way they treated other people, even those who might have looked different from them.

"I hope I was able to show them that there was a different way than the old way," Tony Nathan said. "Even though my hair might be different and the color of my skin might be different, I still have a heart. To grow up in that era, it was like being a part of something that changed the way people thought about things and how they thought about each other."

Former Woodlawn High defensive back Steve Martin remembers having lunch with a few teammates and team chaplain Hank Erwin during the '73 season.

"If I come back in five years, and there are still ten of you guys walking with the Lord, it will be a miracle," Erwin said.

"We were all laughing," Martin said. "He was talking about sixty or seventy guys."

More than a few players who answered Goebel's invitation to accept Jesus Christ as their Lord and Savior in 1973 continued their Christian walk. Gil Wesley, who was the son of Woodlawn High principal Homer Wesley, accepted a football scholarship to Florida State University. He was a three-year starting center for the Seminoles from 1977 to 1979 and was named a three-time All-American. After receiving a master's degree in theology from Dallas Theological Seminary, Wesley became a licensed pastor in Chico, California. He has worked with an organization called The Fellowship and has taken his ministry around the world.

David Davis, who played defensive end on the 1974 team, is a minister, along with his son, and works at the Birmingham Civil Rights Institute. Gary Speers, a defensive end on the 1973 team, earned a football scholarship to Alabama A&M University. He works as a principal at Brownwood Elementary School in

Scottsboro, Alabama, and has pastored at United Methodist and Baptist churches. Steven Washington, who was one of Woodlawn High's first African American football players, is the pastor of a Lutheran church and former athletics director at Concordia College in Selma, Alabama.

"It didn't happen immediately, but I believe that as a result of what happened to us spiritually in 1973 and 1974, these men became ministers in their twenties and thirties," said Greene, who was a longtime talk radio host in Birmingham. "I don't know exactly what happened, but the situation led them to not only make a decision for Christ but to also become ministers."

For many players, the bond the players forged during the 1973 and 1974 seasons would never be broken. When former Colonels linebacker Tommy Rue was shot and killed while working at a carnival in Fort Wayne, Indiana, in July 1977, his mother requested that six of his teammates serve as pallbearers—three blacks and three whites. It seemed a fitting tribute on an otherwise tragic day.

In a prayer letter Goebel wrote shortly after Rue's tragic death, he recalled the young man he'd met at Woodlawn High:

I guess that it would have been about three years ago that God favored my ministry with a very good work among a group of students—many of them athletes from one of our large city schools.

Like most students, they were facing an identity crisis and their problems, some serious, needed a lot of counseling and prayer. Another staff member and I tried to help each one as God gave to us wisdom. I well remember how I used to walk into their gym and in just a few moments how a group of the guys would get with me, ask questions and in general just talk—about the person Jesus. I would look at the coach, not wanting to take any of his time—and he'd just wink, indicating that everything was fine with him. When I finished, I always gave those fellows an opportunity to receive Christ as Savior and meet with me privately. There were always one or two—but with them would be another that I had dealt with before that remained also. I would ask him why he always remained. He would reply—"I just like to hear you talk."

The night they won perhaps the most important football game they had played up until that time, I was asked by one of the coaches to come to the dressing room and have prayer with them. I could never forget the excitement of that evening, after the coach had gotten their attention and I invited them to kneel with me. As I began to pray, I felt a strong, sweaty arm around my neck. As I concluded, I looked up and noticed it was my friend. With tears in his eyes, he said, "Praise the Lord! Jesus let us win!" I answered, "He sure did."

The last time I saw my friend was at an early-morning prayer breakfast. It was the last one for the seniors. As they left, I stood at the door, shaking hands and just rejoicing in my heart as to how many had become truly born-again Christians. Then there he was again—the last one, staying behind. He didn't shake my hand but hugged me around my neck, saying, "Mr. Goebel, I love you and thanks for helping me to find Jesus." I tried to hold back my emotions, but my bigness gave way to my heart, and I just hugged him back and assured him that I loved him also.

I have just read an article in the newspaper about my friend. Somebody has shot and killed him. One bullet through the heart and his life was snuffed out. My condolences go out to his mother, whom he really loved and had mentioned many times to me. She had a very difficult life. I have since prayed for her.

In a way, I am happy for him. I remember a promise Jesus made to all His children, "In my father's house are many mansions, and I go to prepare one for you." Today there is a 20-year-old black boy, rather shy, perhaps still waiting behind all the others, with teeth shining, saying to Jesus, "I really love you."

"They went through a unique time in history," Debbie Gerelds said. "They had to change their way of looking at things. They had to make different judgments than their parents did, after listening to them all their lives. They had a real Christian brotherhood and a relationship with the Lord, their coaches, and each other that was different from a lot of relationships. They wanted as much for each other as they wanted for themselves."

Together, the boys who played on the Woodlawn High football teams in the early 1970s helped a school, community, and a city change for the better. It was a story that transcends football, about how faith triumphed over racial hatred and how love defeated evil. Their dedication to love and unity changed their lives forever.

EPILOGUE

Shortly before his death on January 10, 2003, Tandy Gerelds wrote about his experiences as Woodlawn High School's football coach during the early 1970s:

When I look back on the thirty years I have been in the workforce, I can clearly see how my jobs and environments have affected my personality and how I associate with and treat other people. As a carefree, twenty-two-year-old assistant coach and science teacher, I was probably an extrovert, who cared very much about having friends and being liked. I was not that serious about teaching. I was more concerned with having fun—the more excitement the better. However, even then I took winning very seriously. I never could stand getting beat. During this time, I was very selfish, hardheaded, and could not comfortably express love to others.

After four years of being an assistant under a very demanding head coach and working for a very disciplined principal, I became a little more withdrawn. I started listening and learning more. For the first time, I realized that some people did not work hard and did not have a real drive to succeed.

Six years after I began my educational career, I was put into a leadership position as head coach and athletic director of the third largest high school in Alabama. My decisions now affected many people. For the first time in my life I felt stress and pressure.

The need for success and the drive to be the very best completely engulfed my personality and changed my way of living, both personally and professionally. Professionally, I cared as much about success as I did the young men I was coaching. I became obsessed with competition and winning. Nothing else seemed to fulfill my wants or ego. I considered a defeat a personal flaw in my armor. I decided I wanted to be the very best coach, and I would push my assistant coaches, my players, and myself until I reached my goal. At the same time, I was teaching science. Unfortunately, I was not very interested in science, or, for that matter, the students. However, I did an adequate job of teaching, for fear that my principal or fellow workers would think that I was not doing the job.

I worked about sixteen hours a day. Coaching became an obsession with me. My success came slow and steady, but not near enough to satisfy my inward drive for personal success. I involved myself so deeply in my job that I had very little time for my family or friends. I know now that I was never going to fill the void in my life. I thought it would be filled by winning football games. I did become a good football coach. I learned my lessons from better coaches than myself, who usually beat my team. I learned to be sound at what you do and to have an order of football—or anything else for that matter. I wanted to be well organized and became upset if anything or anyone got out of order.

A series of events transpired in the early 1970s that would forever change my attitudes and behaviors. When I started teaching at Woodlawn High School in Birmingham, Alabama, in 1965, there were no black students in the school. In 1968, a few black students started to school at Woodlawn under the Freedom of Choice Act.

There were no problems in the school, although the black students were not treated sociably. In 1970, Birmingham city schools were forced to integrate. Five hundred black students were transferred from Hayes High School to Woodlawn. The black students did not want to change schools, and the white students did not want them in their school. This led to bad feelings that soon turned to hatred. I was no different than the students. I had never been around black students, and I did not know how to act, coach, or teach them. The only black person that I knew was my maid, Ethel May Porch. Ethel had helped raise me from the time I was three years old. I loved Ethel, but she was the maid and because of her position, she could only be so close to me (my mother made sure she knew her place).

For the next two years, Woodlawn High School became a war zone. Most of the teachers—black and white—quit. Only the strong stayed. The FBI tried to encourage the principal to close the school. He would not. I was attacked, threatened, shot at, and verbally abused constantly. I am saying this all to explain that my attitudes about teaching and coaching were at an all-time low.

I was made assistant principal because no one else would do it, and the principal asked for help. Not surprising, I became a very hardened person, but still had an ego to fill as far as coaching. How was I going to get fifty football players, who did not like each other, to play together and win football games? I went about trying. The harder I tried, the worse it seemed to get.

In August [1973], I decided to have a football camp at the gym, hoping to encourage unity. I was hoping they could learn to get along. I thought if they had a common goal, maybe they could forget their differences and strive together for the team.

After three days of camp, nothing had changed much. The blacks and whites only associated on the practice field. It was at a standstill, as far as how to get the team together. On the third night, just before supper, there was a knock on my office door. In walked a giant of a man, all six feet, four inches and 250 pounds. I asked him what he wanted, and he said he would like to talk to my football players. I, almost angrily, asked him what he wanted to talk about. He told me Jesus Christ. I thought, "Here we go again, someone trying to impose their own beliefs on my kids." I told him I didn't think we would have enough time. He then asked me, "If you died today, would you go to heaven?" I told him I didn't know. He said that I needed to make time for him to speak to the players. I reluctantly gave him thirty minutes after supper.

The man's name was and is Wales Goebel, and he did speak that August night in 1973. I had forty-eight players who had stuck it out. That night, after Wales spoke, forty-four of them became Christians. I was not one of them. I had too much pride to openly admit any weakness. Two weeks later, the team had a Fellowship of Christian Athletes meeting at someone's home. The home was in a very elite section of town. I had been invited by one of the players. As I drove into the Crestwood neighborhood, I had wondered if any of the black kids had ever been in any of these homes before.

As I walked into the house, I noticed black and white boys with their arms around each other. They were laughing and talking in an honest and sincere way. I felt ignored, as if I was not part of the group. After a short stay, I left the party and started home. As I drove home, I began to think about what Wales had said that night. He spoke of being humble and coming to the Lord as a child. When I got home, I got down on my knees and asked the Lord to give me what He gave those kids. I told Him that I didn't care about winning football games and impressing others. All I wanted was to feel like the players felt. The Lord came into my life that night and gave me what He gave the players: love. The Lord did in five seconds what I had tried to do for sixteen hours a day for two years: He made a football team out of individuals.

I know it was a crazy time I went through during the 1970s. Maybe those times tested people more than they are tested today. I do know this: my priorities changed that night and they have been the same ever since. I became the coach I wanted to be and the teacher I should have been. The more I tried to do for other people, the more the Lord would bless me.

A lot of success came my way the next three years: city championships, coach of the year, All-American players, state playoffs. With success come expectations from fans, faculty, friends, and family. Once again, I had to deal with stress and pressure. I always felt that anything that went wrong on the football field was a direct reflection on me. I know now that I put too much pressure on myself. However, I still strive for perfection.

The buildup in pressure seemed to come to its pinnacle in 1974 at Legion Field [in] Birmingham, Alabama. The two schools on the eastern side of Birmingham—Banks and Woodlawn—were both undefeated going into the final game of the year. The consensus was that these were the two best football teams in the state. Also, the two most highly recruited players in the Southeast, Jeff Rutledge and Tony Nathan, would be playing against each other. The tragic irony of the game was that the two teams were in the same area and only one could go to the state playoffs.

The Birmingham media began building the game up three weeks prior to the event. I call it an event because that is what it turned out to be. It was previewed in Sports Illustrated *and was constantly talked about in newspapers and on television. By game time, the Woodlawn and Banks game rivaled Alabama ver-*

sus Auburn. The night we played, Legion Field opened only one gate. [More than forty] thousand people came in. The kickoff was delayed twice so most people could get into the stadium. It was estimated that between ten and twenty thousand people never made it to the gate. There were six Southeastern Conference coaches in the press box, including Paul "Bear" Bryant and Ralph "Shug" Jordan. Eleven players off the two teams went on to play collegiate ball in the Southeastern Conference. Banks beat us 18–7. We didn't go to the playoffs.

I had a hard time accepting the loss to Banks. I cared so much for those great kids. I was ashamed I couldn't give them a way to win. I have always felt that I was cheating kids on the field or in the classroom if I did not give them all I had each day. It takes an enormous amount of energy and enthusiasm to keep performing this way.

One year after the Banks game, I got out of education. I went into the insurance business with my father. I no longer had the enthusiasm I felt I needed to lead young people to a higher level. I have never regretted getting out of coaching in 1975. The business world taught me many lessons that I could not have learned coaching. The greatest lesson it taught me was how to be a good manager. I learned about quality management and that the customer is the most important aspect of any business. I also learned that there were overachievers in the business world, just like in coaching.

I worked at the insurance business very hard and gave it a good shot. However, I never did think that I was as good in business as I was at coaching or teaching young people. After eight years, I had developed a reputation for being a good, honest businessman. I was appointed to the Birmingham Board of Directors for Independent Insurance Agents. I associated with some very successful businessmen and learned a lot about the meaning of success.

During the eight years that I was in the insurance business, I was able to spend time with my wife and three kids that I missed while coaching. I was making a good living and was going to be very successful. My father retired and sold me the business. I didn't have a lot of pressure on me. Now I thought I could relax—wrong! I never could get coaching completely out of my mind. I did not want to be a fool and give up a very stable business, but I had to do what God had given me the ability to do. God, my family, and I—in that order—decided I would get back into education.

After eight years in the insurance business, I had to go back to school at University of Alabama and renew my teaching certificate. After receiving my new certificate, I began to apply for coaching jobs. Eight years is a long time for people to remember someone and what they had accomplished. Obviously, no one broke down the door trying to give me a job.

Bob Haggard, the principal at Deshler High School [in Tuscumbia, Alabama], had coached in Birmingham, and he remembered my name and granted me an interview. Mr. Haggard, Bob Clemmons, the superintendent, and myself seemed to agree on what young people needed and what was best for the school system. I was hired in 1984. The administration showed a lot of faith in hiring me, instead of one of the local people who had applied. The administration took some abuse for hiring me. The administration, however, did not take the abuse that I did. I didn't know how to handle it. This was something new. I had always been well liked, respected, and wanted. People did not like me for the simple reason that I got a job that they wanted someone else to have.

I had come to Tuscumbia with a vision of building a good athletic program, and at the same time raising my family in a wholesome environment. I was hoping to fit into the small town as the coach. *This turned out to be only a vision, not reality. I tried to make friends and be nice to people. I thought that was the answer. I soon found out what most people already knew: you can't please everyone and everyone is not going to like you. My attitudes and approach toward work and people changed. I was spending too much time on the wrong things. I got my priorities back in the order they should have been—God, family, job.*

You find out what kind of person you are during trying times. You have to look at the glass of water as if it is half full, instead of half empty. You have to love God, your family, and the kids or you will never be satisfied in anything you do. God allowed me to win 101 football games in the eleven years I coached at Deshler High. God allowed me to be married to my wife for thirty years and raise three Christian children. I never thought that I deserved the success and blessing that God has given me. I have tried to listen and learn from people who have had more experiences.

Leadership can be a lonely job, but until you get in the arena you will never know how you will react. You need to have the vision and the courage to see it through. You also need wisdom and that only comes from God.